ARGENTINA
The Great Estancias

ARGENTINA
The Great Estancias

EDITED BY

Juan Pablo Queiroz and Tomás de Elia

INTRODUCTION BY

Bonifacio del Carril

TEXT BY

César Aira

PHOTOGRAPHS BY

Tomás de Elia

with additional photography by Cristina Cassinelli de Corral

RIZZOLI
NEW YORK

FRONT COVER: *Avenida de la Cierva, Huetel*

BACK COVER: *The library in the main house at San Miguel*

FRONTISPIECE: *Jardín de la Acequia, Acelain*

First published in the United States of America in 1995 by
RIZZOLI INTERNATIONAL PUBLICATIONS, INC.
300 Park Avenue South, New York, New York 10010

LIBRARY OF CONGRESS CATALOGING-IN-PUBLICATION DATA
Aira, César, 1949–
    Argentina, the great estancias / edited by Juan Pablo Queiroz and
Tomás de Elia ; introduction by Bonifacio del Carril ; text by César Aira ;
photography by Tomás de Elia with additional photography by Cristina
Cassinelli de Corral.
        p.   cm.
        Includes bibliographical references (p.   )
        ISBN 0-8478-1905-1
        1. Architectural photography—Argentina.   2. Haciendas—Argentina
        —Pictorial works.   3. Farmhouses—Argentina—Pictorial works.
I. Queiroz, Juan Pablo.   II. Elia, Tomás de.   III. Title.
TR659.A47   1995   95–8168
779'.482'092—dc20   CIP

ILLUSTRATION CREDITS
All photographs except those noted below by Tomás de Elia.
All numbers refer to page numbers.

Courtesy Enrique Larreta Municipal Museum of Spanish Art, Buenos Aires
© 1995 Artists Rights Society (ARS), New York/VEGAP, Madrid: 90
© 1995 Artists Rights Society, New York (ARS)/SPADEM, Paris: 164
Cristina Cassinelli de Corral: 51, 56, 91, 96–97, 100, 122, 134 (bottom), 136–37, 139,
141, 143, 170–71, 173–75, 195–201
Courtesy Cistercian Abbey of Zwetl, Austria: 11
Courtesy National Museum of Fine Arts, Buenos Aires: 16–17, 142
Courtesy National Historical Museum, Buenos Aires: 22, 138
Courtesy Enrique Larreta Municipal Museum of Spanish Art: 90
Photographic reproductions of art and archival photographs by
Banchero & Caldarella, Buenos Aires.

Text translated from the Spanish by Mario del Carril.

Designed by Marcus Ratliff, Inc.

Printed and bound in Japan

Contents

Acknowledgments

WE WOULD LIKE to acknowledge, above all, the owners of the estancias for their generous hospitality and for making it possible for us to become familiar with the detailed history of their properties. We also extend our appreciation to the staffs of the estancias for their kind cooperation.

With great fondness and respect, we shall remember Bonifacio del Carril, who passed away a short time before we finished this project. He devoted innumerable hours of his time to us, and our lives are truly enriched by his erudition and humanism. We especially thank our friend César Aira for his contribution of texts and literary expertise, and for his infinite patience. To Cristina Cassinelli de Corral, we extend our thanks for her enthusiasm and dedication, and to César Caldarella and Juan Carlos Banchero for their excellent photographic reproductions of the artwork that illustrates this volume.

Our deepest acknowledgments go to all those individuals who believed in this project from the beginning and who followed its progress enthusiastically throughout various stages: Carmen de Iriondo, Pablo Larreta, Nicolás García Uriburu, Teresa de Estrada de Cárcano, Matilde Gyselynck, and Josefina de Iriondo de Atucha.

We would like to acknowledge all those who contributed, in one form or another, to the development of this book: María Cristina Monterubbianesi, Adela Gauna, Bonifacio P. del Carril, Lucía Gálvez de Tiscomia, Yuyú Guzmán, José María Pico, Juan A. González Calderón, María Luisa Herrera Vegas, Jorge Naveiro, Carola Martinez de Hoz de Ramos Mejía, Arch. Jorge O. Gazaneo, Rafael de Oliveira Cézar, Carmen Méndez Duhau de Zuberbühler, José Alfredo Martinez de Hoz, and Alejandro Cordero, Jr.

Our special gratitude goes to the staffs of the libraries of the Sociedad Rural Argentina and the National Academy of History for providing us with the material for our research.

In particular, we thank Jorge Glusberg, Director of the National Museum of Fine Arts; Marta Fernandez, in the Department of Art Conservation; Mercedes di Paola de Picot, Director of the Enrique Larreta Municipal Museum of Spanish Art; María Teresa Dondo de Barcia, Manager of the Department of Museology; and Alfredo I. Barbagallo, Director of the National Historical Museum.

While we are most grateful to all those individuals who offered assistance, we wish to personally acknowledge Miguel and Carlos María Cárcano, Rodolfo de Liechtenstein, Massoumeh Farman-Farmaian, Anita Braun de Biquard, Norberto Padilla, Dinorah Gutiérrez Zaldívar de Larguía, Julio Suaya, Natalia Kohen, Ed Shaw, Ricardo Siri, Jr., Lucrecia de Oliveira Cézar de García Arias; Stella, Viscountess Ednam; Clara Juárez Celman, Mario del Carril, María Teresa Cárdenas Ezcurra, Marcos de Estrada, Jr., Elsa Palilla, Paula Larreta de Ayerza, Sergio M. Ellmann, Azul García Uriburu de Pereda, Amalia Teresa Monterubbianesi; and in Tierra del Fuego, Rae Natalie Prosser de Goodall and Abigail Goodall.

In New York, at Rizzoli International Publications, our most sincere thanks to David A. Morton and Elizabeth White, who supported the project from the start and offered their valuable and expert opinion, and to Megan McFarland for her generous understanding and encouragement. Also in New York, we express special gratitude to Ambassador Guillermo J. McGough, Consul General of Argentina; and to Rita Guibert, Daniel Shapiro, Reinaldo Herrera, Sarah Jane Freymann, Mimí Gonzalez Moreno, Carol Frederick, and in particular, Paulette Villanueva. It was a pleasure to work with the designer, Marcus Ratliff, and his assistant Amy Pyle.

Juan Pablo Queiroz and Tomás de Elia

LEFT: *The main house at Arroyo Dulce, in the province of Buenos Aires.*

Introduction

I N ARGENTINA the extensive rural estates devoted largely to cattle ranching, and to some degree to growing grain, are called *estancias,* and their owners, *estancieros, hacendados* (property owners), or *ganaderos* (cattlemen). The estancias have helped to define the country's spiritual, economic, and social heritage, and it has always been a noble and worthy undertaking to evoke their history and evolution, beginning with the early days of meager resources and a precarious existence.

This book, conceived and compiled by Tomás de Elia and Juan Pablo Queiroz, is a tribute to the estancieros of Argentina, who founded their estancias by braving harsh climates, solitude, and brutal Indian raids (*malones*). The book contains photographs of twenty-two important estancias located throughout the country, with texts by César Aira. It opens with the facade of the church and estancia Santa Catalina, which in the eighteenth century belonged to the Jesuits in Córdoba. The other estancias in the book include two more in the province of Córdoba, one in Mendoza, one in Tucumán, two in Salta, one in Corrientes, eleven in the province of Buenos Aires, two in Tierra del Fuego, and, finally, one in Neuquén.

The first estancias were extensions of a primitive colonial economic institution, the historic *vaquerías* (hunting parties for wild cattle). These vast colonial territories included large tracts of uncultivated land that sustained an enormous number of wild grazing animals called *cimarrones:* bulls, cows, horses, and sheep descended from the animals brought by the Spaniards to the New World that had reproduced amazingly well on the pampa. In the book *Libro de la Montería* of King Alphonse of Castile, published in 1582, Gonçalo Argote de Molina claims that every year more than two hundred thousand hides taken from animals killed in the vaquerías were sent to Seville, in Spain.

Thomas Falkner, the English Jesuit priest who lived in Argentina for nearly forty years—from 1731 until the Jesuits were expelled in 1769—wrote:

There are everywhere very numerous flocks of sheep; and, at my first going thither, the horned cattle were so abundant, that (besides the herds of tame cattle) they ran, in vast droves, wild and without owners; in the plains on both sides of the rivers Paraná, Uruguay; and the river of Plata; and covered all the plains of Buenos-Ayres, Mendoza, Santa Fe, and Cordova....Immense slaughters were made, without more gain than the fat, suet, and hides; the flesh being left to rot. The annual consumption of cattle, slain in this manner alone, in the jurisdiction of this one city and Santa Fe, did not amount to less than some hundreds of thousands....

There is likewise great plenty of tame horses, and a prodigious number of wild ones....The wild horses have no owners, but wander, in great troops, about those vast plains, which are terminated, to the eastward, by the province of Buenos-Ayres and the ocean, as far as the mouth of the Red River; to the westward, by the mountains of Chile and the first Desaguadero; to the north, by the mountains of Cordova, Yacanto, and Rioja; and to the south, by the woods which are the boundaries of the Tehuelhets and Diuihets....In an inland expedition which I made in 1744, being in these plains for the space of three weeks, they were in such vast numbers, that, during a fortnight, they continually surrounded me. Sometimes they passed by me, in thick troops, on full speed, for two or three hours together; during which time, it was with great difficulty that I and

The Hamstringing Knife. Method of Killing Livestock in the Pampas of Buenos Aires. *Etching by Fernando Brambila, Madrid, c. 1798. (Private collection.)*

FACING PAGE, TOP: Indians Plowing, Threshing, and Harvesting Grain. *Within the drawing are notes explaining the procedure. Watercolor by Florián Paucke, c. 1750. (Cistercian Abbey of Zwettl, Austria.)*

FACING PAGE, BOTTOM: Corralling Wild Horses. *Explanatory note within the drawing: "In this manner the Indians hunt the horses with slings and herd them into a hidden corral." Watercolor drawing by Florián Paucke, c. 1750. (Cistercian Abbey of Zwettl, Austria.)*

the four Indians, who accompanied me on this occasion, preserved ourselves from being run over and trampled to pieces by them.

In the presence of such a formidable source of wealth within the reach of anyone who wished to take it, the inhabitants of the first established villages and towns requested permission from the town councils (*cabildos*) to hunt the wild animals, most of which were cattle. In these hunts, groups of men called *accioneros*, armed with *desjarretaderas* (a sharp blade shaped like a half-moon attached to the end of a long spear), felled the animals by cutting the tendons in their hind legs. The animals would fall heavily to the ground and *vaqueros* (cowboys) on foot would quickly cut their throats with long knives, skin the carcasses for hide, strip off the fat, and cut out the tongues for food, leaving the rest for birds of prey and wild dogs.

In this primitive way organized cattle ranching began in the Spanish colonies of America, in spite of the warnings about the dangers of pillaging the herds, which would soon exhaust the supply of livestock. But when the herds were exhausted, the vaqueros of Santa Fe, for example, would

cross over to Entre Ríos and later to Uruguay and continue the hunt. Some of them ventured to settle the land, building thatch-roofed adobe ranchos that eventually dotted the Argentine countryside. These ranchos were the embryonic beginnings of the estancias of Argentina and the Río de la Plata region.

In these early times, when the inhabitants of the countryside were not yet called gauchos, the Jesuits incorporated a great number of cattle into their estancias. In his *Historia de los Abipones* Martín Dobrizhoffer estimates that in Yapeyú the Jesuit fathers had gathered five hundred thousand head of cattle, and in San Miguel even more.

The Jesuit estancias were models for the period and were not limited to raising cattle. The Jesuits introduced agriculture into the colonies by sowing and harvesting wheat on a scale proportionate to the dimensions of their properties. Their harvests provided for the universities, schools, and other institutions they had established in the New World. The *peón,* or agricultural laborer on the estancias, was called *camilucho,* a word derived from the name used to designate servants in Roman convents.

Father Florián Paucke's drawing, made c. 1750, represents several stages of plowing and harvesting wheat. These are almost identical to those described later by Narciso Parchappe in 1827 and in Prilidiano Pueyrredon's watercolor of about 1860. In his sketch narration, the courageous Father Paucke says:

On beautiful days, in the afternoon the Indians bundle the wheat they cut in the morning, placing it on cowhides. Twenty boys on horseback pull these hides to the place the wheat is shredded, piling it on a large, tall stack surrounded by the thick posts of a stockade. Forty or more horses, usually mares, are brought into the enclosure, which is then closed, and the horses are driven around by whips. Little by little the large stack of wheat is reduced under the feet of the animals until all that was straw becomes undone, trampled underfoot, and the grain has been separated. After the thicker husks are eliminated from the wheat, other Indians pull it to another connected enclosure, where the shredded wheat is cleansed by throwing it in the air. It is then placed in strongly stitched leather bags.

In other sketches Father Paucke shows a curious aspect of life on a Jesuit estancia. After the wheat had been harvested, Paucke's custom was to permit the Indians and their chiefs to hunt wild horses in the countryside for the same number of days they had worked in the harvest. The Indians preferred this arrangement to any other form of payment. According to what Father Paucke has written on the sketch, the Indians would drive the wild horses into enclosures hidden in the woods, where they could be easily corralled.

At the end of the eighteenth century, as a consequence of the expulsion of the Jesuits, cattle-raising in the colonies reached a critical juncture as the number of estancias owned by lay people increased. In 1809 Félix de Azara wrote:

> The pastors or owners of herds of cattle are busy taking care of twelve million head of cattle and three million horses and a considerable number of sheep. That is my estimate of the domesticated animals in these regions. A sixth of the herds belong to the government of Paraguay, and the rest to Buenos Aires. I don't include in these numbers two million wild cattle, or cimarrones, that might be found in the countryside, nor the innumerable wild horses.

The French savant Alcide D'Orbigny was probably the most thorough observer of the estancia in the first part of the nineteenth century. He was a young naturalist who traveled in South America between 1826 and 1833, and later wrote a monumental nine-volume work that includes more than four hundred illustrations of his travels based on his own sketches.

In the first volume of his *Partie Historique*, D'Orbigny meticulously describes the estancia Rincón de Luna in the province of Corrientes, which he visited in June 1827 accompanied by Parchappe. The estancia was situated on a slice of land between two tributaries of the river Batel; it was sixty-nine miles long and three-and-a-half miles wide, and was formerly part of an old Jesuit estate. The estancia included the house of the estanciero, a few *puestos* (outlying buildings for the ranch-hands), and a small chapel. The estancias near the city of Buenos Aires, observed D'Orbigny, had between thirty and forty thousand head of cattle each, while the estancia of Rincón de Luna in Corrientes had six

thousand cows, oxen, and bulls, without counting two hundred horses and eight hundred sheep.

The main house consisted of three rooms. The first was the living quarters of the estanciero; the second room was the kitchen where the ranch-hands slept in winter because it was heated by a chimneyless cooking stove called a *fogón*. In summer the ranch-hands would sleep under palm trees in an enormous grove. Hides and fat were stored in the third room, according to D'Orbigny. The English sailor Emeric E. Vidal, who was in the Río de la Plata region between 1816 and 1818, said that sometimes these three rooms were built separately.

D'Orbigny wrote that when there were trees on an estancia, immense round corrals were built near the houses, as stockades with posts driven into the ground next to each other. Rincón de Luna had two stockades built with stakes made from the trunks of palm trees that had been split down the middle. One of these stockades was large enough to pen all the cattle, the other held all the horses. In another corral they enclosed the sheep.

The Genevese lithographer César Hipólito Bacle seems to have used D'Orbigny's description of Rincón de Luna to compose an interesting color lithograph, included in the sixth book of the collection *Trages y Costumbres de la Provincia de Buenos-Ayres* (Costumes and Customs of the Province of Buenos Aires), published in 1833. It shows everything described by D'Orbigny: to the right, the owner's house; in the center, the livestock in the fields, two corrals constructed as stockades, both of them round, one with horses and the other with cows. Below there is a scene of a roundup.

Parchappe pointed out that in Buenos Aires corrals were surrounded by deep trenches to protect against Indian attacks. Trenches were also dug in a square around the living quarters, and one or two cannons were used to scare the Indians. When wood wasn't available trenches were used to construct makeshift corrals to replace the traditional stockades; these trenches would be placed near those that protected the houses. Except for these details, according to Parchappe, the houses of the estancieros of the province of Buenos Aires were like those in Corrientes and other parts of the country.

Finally D'Orbigny observed that when there were too many animals, the estancias were divided into several puestos, workstations or outposts in which a ranch hand lived alone or with his family and where he carried out the responsibility of caring for the nearby cattle. In general mares were not sold; they were used only to provide horses for the estancias, or when there were too many, they were killed for their hides.

The main types of work carried out in the estancias were breaking-in horses, branding animals, and the roundup. Toward the end of the nineteenth century agricultural tasks were added to this list. In 1833 the world renowned naturalist Charles Darwin wrote a classic description of the breaking-in of horses:

One evening a *domador* (a tamer of horses) came for the purpose of breaking-in some colts. I will describe the preparatory steps, for I believe they have not been mentioned by other travellers.

A troop of wild young horses is driven into a corral, or large enclosure of stakes, and the door is shut. We will suppose that one man alone has to catch and mount a horse which as yet had never felt bridle or saddle. I believe that, except by a gaucho, such a feat would be utterly impracticable. The gaucho picks out a full-grown colt and as the beast rushes around the circus, he throws his lasso so as to catch both front legs. Instantly the horse rolls over with a heavy shock, and while struggling on the ground, the gaucho, holding the lasso tight, makes a circle so as to catch one of the hind legs just beneath the fetlock and draws it close to the two front legs; he then hitches the lasso so that the three are bound together. Then, sitting on the horse's neck, he fixes a strong bridle without a bit to the lower jaw; this he does by passing a narrow thong through the eye holds at the end of the reins, and several times round both jaws and tongue. The two front legs are now tied closely together with a leather thong fastened by a slipknot. The lasso which bound the three together being then loosened, the horse rises with difficulty.

The gaucho, now holding fast the bridle fixed to the lower jaw, leads the horse outside the corral. If a second man is present (otherwise the trouble is much greater) he holds the animal's head, while the first puts

Estancia in the Province of Buenos Aires. *Colored lithograph. (Private collection.) Black and white original printed in Bacle y Ca.,* Trages y Costumbres de la Provincia de Buenos-Ayres *(Buenos Aires, 1833).*

on the horse cloths and saddle and girths all together. During this operation, the horse, from dread and astonishment at thus being bound round the waist, throws himself over and over again on the ground, and till beaten and unwilling to rise. At last, when the saddling is finished, the poor animal can hardly breathe for fear, and is white with foam and sweat.

The man now prepares to mount by pressing heavily on the stirrup, so that the horse may not lose its balance, and at the moment that he throws his leg over the animal's back, he pulls the slipknot binding the front legs, and the beast is free. Some horsebreakers pull the knot while the animal is lying on the ground, and standing over the saddle, allow him to rise beneath them. The horse, wild with dread, gives a few more violent bounds, and then starts off at full gallop; when quite exhausted the man, by patience, brings him back to the corral, where, reeking hot and scarcely alive, the poor beast is let free. Those animals which will not gallop away, but obstinately throw themselves on the ground, are by far the most troublesome.

This process is tremendously severe, but in two or three trials the horse is tamed. It is not, however, for some weeks that the animal is ridden with the iron bit and solid ring, for it must learn to associate the will of the rider with the feel of the rein before the more powerful bridle can be of service.

In his painting, the Uruguayan artist Juan Manuel Blanes realistically and vividly portrays the culminating

The Horse-Breaking. *Oil*
painting by Juan Manuel Blanes,
1865. (Private collection.)

moment of the *doma* (horse-breaking). The *domador's* strength and the expression on his face are truly remarkable.

The *rodeo* (the gathering of cattle in a chosen place in an open plain) was essential to the work of the estanciero. The animals would be taken to a site to which they were accustomed and could recognize by tracks they had left from previous rodeos. Domesticated cattle would also be led there as a lure to attract the wild cattle (cimarrones) and the *alzados,* the tame animals that had become wild again.

A painting by Pueyrredon shows the details of a roundup on the immense *pampa* (plains). To the left foreground are the estanciero and his foreman instructing the gaucho-ranch-hand as he adjusts the girth of his mount before going to carry out his orders.

When the animals belonging to one cattleman strayed into the herd of another, the first could request a roundup to separate the herds; the roundup was undertaken by the person who accepted the request. But rodeos also took place before beginning other kinds of work on the estancia. The act of gathering the cattle was called *volteada,* in which the cowhands rode on horseback after scattered animals to bring them to the roundup. Gaucho-ranch-hands were experts in this type of work, and, according to Carlos E. Pellegrini, they were paid extra for it.

A memoir signed by José M. Jurado, and published in 1875 by the Sociedad Rural Argentina (Argentina's earliest and most prestigious cattlemen's association), describes the main features of life on the primitive estancias of Buenos Aires. In this document, Jurado remarks that rodeos began with a group of tame animals, called the *señuelo* (lead cows). But if the operation was poorly executed, or the lure did not work, there was always the risk that the cattle would be dispersed. Jurado adds that on many occasions, after a failed volteada, or a poorly executed rodeo, the owner of an estancia that had fifteen or twenty thousand head of cattle might find himself with nothing at the end of the day.

No one has described branding with greater accuracy and detail than D'Orbigny on his visit to Rincón de Luna. He tells us that the estanciero constructed a narrow passageway, shaped like a funnel and made with wooden stakes, that permitted the animals to pass single file. As the cattle emerged on the other side of this passageway, those that had not been branded were separated from the rest. The riders slowly circled the cattle, swinging their lassos into shape until they threw them over an animal's horns, then, reining in their mount and offering its flank to the bull, they would hold the lasso taut to contain the animal's fierce charge as it attempted to escape. Ranch-hands on foot would lasso the animal's feet and trip it to the ground, assisted by other ranch-hands, who would throw the animal on its side by twisting its tail while avoiding its desperate kicks. Another man would sit on the steer's head to keep it still as it bellowed in pain, while a gaucho would apply a red-hot branding iron to its rump, middle ribs, or loins, according to the owner's custom.

A cattleman's registered brand was usually formed by the initial of his last name surrounded by a floral design to distinguish it from other brands with the same initial. Some cowhands memorized all the features of a brand name and could recognize it at a distance.

In colonial times agricultural work, as opposed to ranching, was performed mostly by black slaves; however, Indian slaves were used on the Jesuit estancias. The gaucho, who had been born and raised on a horse, did not like to work on his feet. However, in the nineteenth century some gauchos did help to sow and harvest grain, continuing a practice already described and commonly followed on the Jesuit estancias. The gauchos preferred to do everything on a horse; for the farm work they would use mares, sometimes one hundred at a time, to step on stalks of grain to separate it from the straw.

On the primitive estancias sheep shearing was a very important activity and was carried out by women and young gauchos. The industry truly developed after Juan Harrat introduced Merinos, a breed of sheep, into the Río de la Plata region. According to Pellegrini, the estancias had enormous flocks of sheep, and selling wool became one of their main sources of income.

Two resources an estancia required in the eighteenth and first part of the nineteenth century were water and salt. If an estancia was near a permanent water source, such as a river, stream or lagoon, it did not have a problem; otherwise its situation was precarious. The only way of obtaining the little water that was available was by means of a leather bucket called a *pelota* (ball), which would be dropped into a well. The gaucho would raise and lower

FOLLOWING PAGES:
The Rodeo. *Oil painting by Prilidiano Pueyrredon, 1861. (National Museum of Fine Arts, Buenos Aires.)*

Group of Horse Carts.
Watercolor by Carlos E. Pellegrini,
1831. Originally appeared in
Pellegrini, Tableau Pittoresque
de Buenos-Ayres *(Buenos*
Aires, 1831). (Private collection.)

were protected en route by the frontier military forces. In 1828, when Pellegrini arrived in Buenos Aires, he witnessed the striking spectacle of a five hundred-wagon-caravan ready to dispatch to the pampa. It was an expedition similar in all respects to those formed yearly to bring back salt. A vast number of old two-wheeled carts with immense wheels, each drawn by six oxen, lined up in a caravan. Three thousand oxen would participate in such a trek together with the gauchos that led each team. According to Pellegrini, the wagon painted with the national colors (blue and white) in the foreground of his picture belonged to the foreman.

In 1840 Don Luis Vernet, the former governor of the Malvinas, invented a potion that was very successful in protecting hides from being spoiled by moths; it became an indispensable tool for the cattlemen, keeping their hides intact until they were shipped.

Around 1870 the European immigrant farmers cultivated, on a large scale, the vast natural grasslands. Italians were the first to do so, as they settled in great expanses of virgin land. In seventy years, the relatively brief period between 1870 and 1940, Argentina's population increased from eight hundred thousand to thirteen million, a demographic fact that contributed greatly to changing the nature of country life. Some immigrants made it rich, others did not; but they all worked hard to improve their living conditions with the help of the most modern and sophisticated agricultural machinery, promoting progress and increasing the number of estancias.

But time did not pass in vain. The estancia began to provide permanent quarters for many gauchos who abandoned their nomadic ways and settled down to take on steady work. This transformation of the colonial estancias, as they were described to us by D'Orbigny, was both decisive and significant. A new concept of the estancia predominated that did not modify the essence of the old. Rincón de López is a typical example. This estancia on the Salado river began as a Jesuit Indian settlement (*reducción*) known as Nuestra Señora de la Concepción de las Pampas (Our Lady of Conception of the Pampas). In the 1760s it was occupied by the López de Osornio family, ancestors of Juan Manuel de Rosas. Today the old colonial ranch house has been transformed into a comfortable country house. The

the bucket with a rope tied to the girth of his saddle, as noted by Azara. But very little water could be obtained in that way.

In the *Revista del Plata* (1853) Pellegrini describes a "rural hydraulic machine" that became essential to life on estancias without nearby water in the early part of the nineteenth century. The machine was invented by the Spaniard Lanuze in 1823 and was called the "bucket without a bottom." It consisted of a whole colt's hide, obtained by cutting crosswise along the loins and throat so that it resembled a sort of leather pipe with openings at either end. One of the openings drew water, the other collected the runoff. It can be seen in a lithograph by Pellegrini, which portrays the well and the horse that pulls the bucket. Pellegrini, who was a careful observer of life in the country, wrote that the bucket without a bottom could provide water to a herd of two thousand head of cattle during a summer.

Salt was also essential to cattlemen and to the *saladeros* (salting plants) that prepared *charquí* (jerked beef) and hides for export; these establishments increased in number in the early nineteenth century. Every year large wagon expeditions took off for Salinas Grandes or Patagonia to bring back salt. These expeditions, which traversed Indian country,

Estancia of Don Manuel Lynch in the Province of Buenos Aires. *Watercolor by Prilidiano Pueyrredon, 1870. (Private collection.)*

narrow posts on the veranda have been replaced by thick, round brick columns. The house continues to have only one inhabited floor, while the *mangrullo* (the primitive watchtower southern estancias needed to guard against surprise Indian attacks) has been replaced by a *mirador* (an enclosed overlook similar to those found in the houses of Yankee skippers on the New England coastline and sometimes called a widow's walk). The architectural style was converted from colonial to *criollo* (creole), a style whose virtues were noticed by the celebrated French architect Le Corbusier when he visited Buenos Aires in 1929.

Other estancieros, instead of transforming the old structures, built recreational homes or chalets on their estancias like those being built at that time in Mar del Plata, a seaside resort. One luxury perpetrated others, and the architectural development of the Argentine estancia evolved into the construction of grand European-style mansions. Tempted by the great fortunes their lands were worth and the great sums they yielded, a significant group of estancieros began to build great houses, true rural palaces of European inspiration that even today preserve the beauty of their lines without altering the old creole traditions.

General Justo José de Urquiza pioneered this development. A few years before he became president, Urquiza built on his estancia San José, near Concepción del Uruguay in the province of Entre Ríos, a great palace that is now a museum. The Italian architects Jacinto Dellepiane and Pedro Fossati worked successively on the project, whose construction began in 1848. The American captain Thomas J. Page, who visited San José in 1853, said that on the enormous undulating plain that surrounds the palace, which boasts two great towers, no less than seventy thousand sheep, forty thousand head of cattle and two thousand horses grazed. The aerial view of the mansion and surrounding plantations was depicted in a lithograph by Lemercier in Paris, according to Arnoult's drawing, and was published in 1858 in the Belgian baron Alfred M. Du Graty's book on the Argentine confederation (see page 8).

In this way the Argentine estanciero fulfilled his mission as a producer and disseminator of culture. But this introduction would not be complete without a brief reference to the gaucho-ranch-hand, servant and friend of the landowner, who worked tirelessly to build and develop the estancias. Nor should the nomadic gaucho be forgotten, he who loved his freedom and wandered the pampas,

Gaucho with His Horse. *Oil painting by Raymond Q. Monvoisin, 1842. (Private collection.)*

always working on specialized tasks and scouting for travelers who ventured to cross the grasslands. This gaucho would come, dressed in his best clothes and mounted on his best horse, to the large countryside gatherings—the domas, roundups, and brandings—to demonstrate his skills with the lasso and *boleadoras* (lariat), as Sarmiento recalls in an unforgettable page in *Facundo*, his book describing the life of the gaucho in the early nineteenth century.

In 1842 the French painter Raymond Quinsac Monvoisin, the most important artist to travel through Argentina in the nineteenth century, painted a magnificent full-length portrait of a gaucho-ranch-hand on an estancia. This painting, one of his great masterworks, says everything. The gaucho's face has a slightly Moorish air and a firmness of expression. He wears the typical truncated cone hat and a large yellowish kerchief knotted under his chin, along with a large, ostentatious poncho *patria* with wide red and blue stripes from which emerge the white sleeves of his shirt. The *chiripá* (an embroidered, worsted shawl worn around the waist, drawn between the legs over lace pantaloons) is rolled up over his undergarments, which are decorated with fringe, and his boots, made of colt-hide, are open in front. In his right hand he holds a *porteño* (from Buenos Aires) leather whip with a short handle, and in his left he holds the reins of his dark chestnut horse. The horse's bridle has a headdress with red tassels, and its tail is tied in a double knot. In the painting the horse's figure surrounds the gaucho as though to protect him.

Each estancia has its own soul, and this brief history defines the spiritual substance of the Argentine estancias. The essential aspects of rural life in Argentina have been outlined, beginning with the vaquerías of the early days and including the days of splendor, when cattle ranching and farming were the country's main sources of material and moral wealth.

Bonifacio del Carril
Member of the National Academy of History
National Academy of Fine Arts

Santa Catalina

Juan Kronfuss. Bird's-eye view of the church and former convent of estancia Santa Catalina, *1920. (National Historical Museum, Buenos Aires.)*

FACING PAGE: *Partial view of the Patio of Honor and mountainous landscape from the roof of the church. The estancia occupies more than seventeen hundred acres of land and is isolated from neighboring settlements.*

Presiding over the church altarpiece of gilded carob wood is a polychromed figure of Santa Catalina. The objects of worship are all original to the church.

FACING PAGE: *Facade of the Jesuit church of Santa Catalina, constructed in the mid-eighteenth century. Because the facade includes German baroque elements, it is thought that the architect was a German priest, Antonio Harls.*

A LABYRINTH of wild and picturesque valleys extends northeast of the provincial capital of Córdoba. There, a traveler following the old dirt road past the town of Jesús María comes upon Santa Catalina, the center of Jesuit missionary work in Argentina in the seventeenth and eighteenth centuries. During that period, the Society of Jesus, the religious order founded by St. Ignatius Loyola, became the largest landowner in the territory under the Spanish viceroyalty. Its presence left an indelible imprint along the rivers that run from Paraguay into the Río de la Plata, and in Alto Perú (now Bolivia), Cuyo, and especially Córdoba, where the Jesuits arrived in 1586.

Santa Catalina's striking buildings—a colonial church and an imposing house—are among the most important and best preserved legacies of their tenure in Argentina. The Jesuits acquired Santa Catalina from Luis Frasson, a blacksmith, in 1622. Eventually the lands extended to four hundred thousand acres and the crops and livestock supported the Society's schools and universities. A 1760 inventory mentions 406 slaves, twelve thousand cows, six thousand sheep and an equal number of mules, as well as looms and mills. The Jesuits made important improvements; among these was an underground aqueduct built in 1656 to bring water from the mountains of Ongamira to a reservoir near the original buildings.

A window of the colonial-style house. Santa Catalina is one of the most important and best preserved architectural works completed by the Society of Jesus during its tenure under the Spanish viceroyalty.

FACING PAGE: *The pulpit, a confessional, and a balcony reserved for Jesuit fathers attending Mass.*

Construction of the church began in the mid-eighteenth century, and no one is certain who designed it, but it is thought that the architect was Father Antonio Harls. He was born in Bavaria, which would explain the building's German baroque features. The cloisters and adjoining buildings were built a short time later.

The facade of the church is exceptionally sober and harmonious; but inside, the main altar of gilded carob wood is intricately carved, with a sculpture of Santa Catalina above. Slaves and Indians heard Mass in the nave, while two balconies were reserved for the Jesuits. The cemetery next to the church contains the tomb of Doménico Zipoli, an important eighteenth-century Italian musician who composed a considerable amount of his work in the Americas. The house complex was built around three courtyards: the master bedrooms and the parlors opened onto the main patio; the workshops and quarters of ranch-hands and artisans surrounded the second; and in the last were the stables.

The Jesuits were expelled from the Spanish viceroyalty in 1769. Five years later the Junta de Temporalidades, the body that administered the properties of the Society of Jesus, sold Santa Catalina to Don Francisco Antonio Díaz, the mayor of Córdoba. In the bill of sale Díaz made the commitment to maintain the church "with appropriate decency, and to assume all costs of candles, wine and anything else necessary for its utmost preservation."

José Javier Díaz, son of Francisco Antonio, was twice elected governor of Córdoba. Other members of his family became governors, ministers, judges, senators, and deputies. The family held so many public posts that there was talk of a Clan of Santa Catalina, with political influence on a provincial and national scale.

The Santa Catalina property has changed over time as the land has been subdivided and passed down through

One of the arcades surrounding the central courtyard. Originally, the Jesuits' bedrooms and parlors opened onto these corridors. Today, the rooms belong to the descendants of Francisco Antonio Díaz, who acquired the estancia in 1774.

LEFT: *Entrance to the Patio of Honor.*

The seminary, a separate part of the complex, where students of the Society of Jesus lived during the summer. Throughout the rest of the year the building lodged the estancia's unmarried female slaves.

FACING PAGE: *Seminary arcade.*

generations, but the church has been not been altered. Although some of its original artistic treasures were stolen during the civil wars in the early nineteenth century, many remain. Santa Catalina is exceptionally well preserved and reflects the commitment of the family that has owned the property for more than two hundred years and has honored the terms of the original sale.

Today the estancia includes more than seventeen hundred acres, and the neighboring estancias, whose lands were once part of the original Santa Catalina, also belong to descendants of Francisco Antonio Díaz.

La Paz

Argentine president Julio A. Roca, with his daughters and a group of friends, pose in front of La Paz's main house at the turn of the century. President Roca modernized the house around 1890 and used it as his summer residence. (Private collection.)

FACING PAGE: Native tipa trees border the lake along the entrance drive to the house. The park was designed by the French landscape architect Charles Thays around 1903.

THE MOUNTAINOUS TERRAIN of Ascochinga, thirty miles north of the city of Córdoba, is the site of this idyllic estancia. La Paz was originally part of Santa Catalina, the vast Jesuit estancia of 460 thousand acres that Francisco Antonio Díaz bought after Spain expelled the Jesuits from its colonies. After Díaz's death, the land was subdivided, and the parcel now called La Paz became the property of Tomás Funes, who was married to Díaz's granddaughter. Funes was active in Córdoba politics, and when he heard that the pact of San José de Flores had been signed on November 11, 1859, ending the civil wars and establishing peace in the republic, he decided to change the name of his estancia from Corral de Piedra (Stone Corral) to La Paz (Peace).

In 1872 both of Tomás Funes's daughters married future Argentine presidents: Elisa married Miguel Juárez Celman of Córdoba, and Clara married Julio Argentino Roca, from the province of Tucumán. Clara inherited La Paz and spent many summers there with her husband and children.

Julio Roca was appointed Minister of War and Navy in 1877 by President Nicolás Avellaneda. Two years later he successfully led the so-called Desert Campaign, which eliminated the Indian threat and opened up several million acres of fertile land for agriculture. In 1880 Roca became president for the first time, and in 1898 he was elected again—the only Argentine president to be elected twice and to complete his second term.

When Clara Funes died in 1890, Roca inherited the estancia. He used it primarily as a country house, although as a cattle breeder, he focused his efforts on La Paz and two of his other estancias in the province of Buenos Aires: La Larga (The Expanse) and La Argentina. It was said that the names of his three estancias expressed his generation's desire for long-term peace in Argentina.

The main house includes parts of the original building that date from the early nineteenth century, and has some adobe walls that are more than thirty inches thick. In the 1890s Roca modernized the house, and in 1903 he comissioned the French landscape architect Charles Thays to design the park. Today the great lake in the park is surrounded by native *tipa* trees, plane trees, oaks, and century-old eucalyptuses. About a hundred yards from the main house was a small building with an elegant wood-panelled room that Roca commissioned as a *salon*, used for parties by his five daughters and their relatives and friends. The entry stairs led to a balcony completely surrounding the interior, which was furnished with sofas and a grand piano to accompany singing and dancing to the waltzes, quadrilles, and mazurkas fashionable at that time.

The Jesuits built more than six miles of irrigation channels at La Paz that are no longer in use, but old Indian artifacts are carefully preserved on the estancia, including stones carved into concave vessels that were used for grinding corn into meal.

San Miguel

View of the park and sierras surrounding San Miguel. An irrigation system built by the Jesuits provides water for the gardens.

FACING PAGE: *Master bedroom wing of the house. The estancia is located in the isolated San Miguel valley in the northern part of Córdoba.*

Detail of the rustic doors of the main house.

THIS ESTANCIA LIES in the isolated San Miguel valley in the northern part of Córdoba. In the eighteenth century it was a *puesto* (outpost) on the vast Jesuit property of Santa Catalina. Under Jesuit direction, the Indians constructed many miles of dry stone walls that can still be seen winding over the hills. They also built an irrigation system and a number of stone corrals, one of which stands a few yards from the main house and continues to be used for working with the herd of cattle that grazes on San Miguel's ten thousand acres of land.

Throughout most of the nineteenth century San Miguel's owners were British. In 1925, the Schieles sold the estancia to Miguel Angel Cárcano and his wife, Stella de Morra, through their manager, Hugo Backhouse. In his memoir *Among the Gauchos*, Backhouse recalls his life at San Miguel at the turn of the century:

> The house was built by the Jesuits many years ago and was made of adobe bricks. . . . Standing on the veranda one looked down over the garden, which sloped gently away. . . . At the back of the house there were pine trees, giving the background for the house, with the peak rising immediately behind them. A wonderful setting,

Sharing an informal moment at San Miguel in 1931 are, from left, Edward, Prince of Wales; Prince George (later Duke of Kent), María Teresa Bosch Alvear de Dodero, and Stella de Morra de Cárcano, owner of the estancia. (Private collection.)

Jacqueline Bouvier Kennedy on horseback during her stay at San Miguel in April, 1966. (Private collection.)

LEFT: *San Miguel's library contains many splendidly bound volumes on history and an important collection of newspapers and periodicals from the nineteenth century. The ceiling is covered with a Philippe de Lascelle design in chintz. Flanking the entrance are two Hindu ceremonial trumpets, a gift from Indian Prime Minister Nehru to Miguel Angel Cárcano.*

and although I lived here for a number of years I never tired of admiring the beauty of this place.

Backhouse lived in the original house, of whose primitive features he wrote:

(They) fitted in with the vastness of the surrounding country, which rose to a height of seven thousand feet with its grass-covered hilltops, deep ravines and innumerable streams that flowed into the larger rivers below, whose waters were plentifully stocked with trout. Cattle and horses were grazing in the most unusual places and I kept wondering how they got up there or how they could get down again.

The Cárcanos became familiar with San Miguel during vacations at nearby La Cumbre. While riding in the mountains they were impressed by the beauty of the place and, after touring the property with Backhouse, decided to buy it.

Miguel Angel Cárcano belonged to a prominent family from Córdoba. His father, Don Ramón, served twice as governor of the province. Stella de Morra was the great-granddaughter of Justo José de Urquiza, the first constitutional president of Argentina. Cárcano achieved success as a diplomat, a politician, and a historian. He was Minister of Foreign Relations and Minister of Agriculture, and like his father, he became president of the National Academy of History. During World War II, Cárcano was the Argentine Ambassador in London. He had two daughters and one son: Stella, Viscountess Ednam; the Honorable Ana Inés Astor; and Miguel Angel (Michael) Cárcano. Michael recalls arriving at San Miguel when he was a child, before roads were built, riding on the back of a mule with his mother and a Scottish governess.

The Cárcanos built roads shortly after they bought the property and constructed a house on the original site using stones taken from the San Miguel river and hand cut. They planted trees and flowers, always taking care not to alter the rugged, unspoiled landscape. The Prince of Wales visited San Miguel in 1931, accompanied by Prince George, who described it as a haven of rest; John F. Kennedy came in 1941, and years later his widow, Jacqueline, with her two children. Cecil Beaton, who visited in 1971, left a detailed

A smaller library, adjacent to the main living room.

LEFT: *In the dining room, Georgian boiserie of pine purchased by the Cárcanos in London during World War II. The carved wooden doors date from the Jesuit period in the eighteenth century.*

Riding in a stone corral near the house are, from left: Don Manuel Avanza, Osvaldo Moyano, Carlos María Cárcano, and Héctor Guzmán.

FACING PAGE: *The "stone sitting room." Above the fireplace are eighteenth-century French paintings; on the side table, a childhood portrait of Miguel Cárcano III by his aunt, Chiquita Astor.*

account of his impressions in his memoir *The Parting Years*. He gave equal praise to the landscape and the house, and his favorite room was the library, which contains a collection of the first newspapers published in Argentina and splendidly bound volumes. Such juxtaposition of culture and wilderness has always been the hallmark of San Miguel.

Today, San Miguel belongs to Miguel and Carlos María Cárcano, sons of Michael Cárcano and Teresa de Estrada. Together with their mother, they carry on the family tradition of hospitality and devotion to the land.

The San Miguel river flows through the property, falling into a natural pool called La Taza (The Cup), a landscape feature typical in the province of Córdoba.

The estancia's park winds through the valley without disturbing its rugged natural landscape. In the foreground and background are dry stone walls built by Indians in the eighteenth century, under the direction of the Jesuits.

Los Alamos

A statue of the Virgin transforms the main courtyard into a peaceful enclave. According to legend, an Indian chief was hanged here during a raid in 1838.

FACING PAGE: *The main house was built in 1830 as a frontier fort. Its thick adobe walls, interior courtyard, and barred windows offered protection against Indian raids and remain intact today.*

Entrance to the main house. Shade trees were planted nearby to provide relief from summer heat. The entrance gate replaces an old wooden portal that sealed off the house during Indian raids.

RIGHT: *A Paraguayan hammock in the main courtyard, an inviting retreat during an afternoon siesta.*

Los ALAMOS, property of the Aldao Bombal family, is about twenty miles from the city of San Rafael, 125 miles south of the provincial capital of Mendoza. About 1760, Juan Bombal, the son of a French officer who had come to the country at the beginning of the eighteenth century, established himself in this province. His grandson Domingo Bombal Ugarte, a prominent citizen and prosperous cattleman, married Nemesia Videla, a member of an old Mendoza family, and bought Los Alamos in 1866.

The large house was built around 1830 as a frontier fort. The structure had thick adobe walls, an interior courtyard, windows with handwrought iron grates, and a dry moat for defense against Indian raids. During the nineteenth century, the estancia resisted two Indian invasions in which women were kidnapped and cattle were stolen. According to oral tradition, an Indian chief was hanged in the main courtyard of the house as a reprisal. The 1838 attack, which involved the entire region, was recorded in several sketches and paintings by the German artist Johann Moritz Rugendas, who was traveling through Mendoza at the time.

Los Alamos added to Domingo Bombal's already extensive holdings in the province. He established four staging posts to shorten the trip between the estancia and the city of Mendoza, but his political career robbed attention from Los Alamos. On several occasions Bombal was temporary governor of Mendoza; he became absorbed with rebuilding

The "mirror room" displays antique etchings of ladies dressed in typical fashions of the time. The writer Susana Bombal decorated Los Alamos and created the estancia's present character.

LEFT: Plants, clay pots and vases, and a wrought iron spiral staircase evoke the estancia's simplicity and natural ambiance.

Johann Moritz Rugendas. Drawing depicting the abduction of a female settler during an attack by Pehuenche Indians in the San Rafael area, which includes Los Alamos. 1838. (Private collection.)

the city, which was devastated by an earthquake of 1861 that took his wife and three of his children. The task of developing the estancia was left to his youngest son, Domingo Evaristo Bombal. The younger Bombal made Los Alamos his home, planting vineyards and raising cattle to sell locally and in Chile.

Early in the twentieth century, when the railroad linked Mendoza and Buenos Aires, the provincial economy turned around: cattle breeding was largely replaced by the cultivation of fruit that could now be shipped fresh by train to Buenos Aires. Most important, there was a growing market in Buenos Aires for wines from Mendoza and San Juan, due to the ban on European imports during World War I.

Domingo Evaristo Bombal was unable to take advantage of this turn of events—he died prematurely in Los Alamos in 1908. His wife, Susana Hughes, and their three daughters moved to Buenos Aires and rented out the land. The house was uninhabited for twenty years until

one of the daughters, Susana Bombal, a distinguished writer, returned and began to restore the building. Without modifying its remaining original traces, she gave the estancia the character it has today. The house is typically *criollo* (creole), one of the few of its kind that remain in the province, as well as one of the oldest, having survived numerous earthquakes. Susana Bombal converted the house into a refuge for writers and artists, among them Jorge Luis Borges, Manuel Mujica Lainez, and Richard Llewellyn.

Today the estancia belongs to Susana Bombal's nephews. Its twelve thousand acres are densely cultivated with fruit trees and grapevines; the wine produced is exported primarily to Belgium and the Netherlands.

LEFT: *The "glass room" is the brightest space in the house. Above the fireplace are copper utensils and antique branding irons formerly used on the estancia.*

*Susana Bombal transformed
Los Alamos into a refuge for writers
and artists. Her studio occupies
the oldest room in the house, where
she wrote most of her works. The
floor is inlaid with trunks of fruit
trees that grow on the estancia;
on the ceiling are plaster beams made
by Araucanian Indians.*

RIGHT: *The dining room has
a stone floor and thick adobe walls,
Portuguese chairs, an antique
scale transformed into a chandelier,
and a large fireplace used during
the cold winters.*

El Churqui

Llamas wander across El Churqui's solitary, silent landscape. The estancia was founded in 1776 and encompasses forty thousand acres.

FACING PAGE: *The master bedroom viewed from the gallery. On the thatched roof, cane reeds anchor straw that extends over the eaves.*

With its thick adobe walls, the house sits atop a hill and dominates the valley. El Churqui is one of the most traditional estancias in Tucumán province.

FACING PAGE: *El Churqui's main house, owned by the Zavaleta family for two centuries, stands before an impressive backdrop of mountain ranges in the Tafi valley.*

EL CHURQUI, in the province of Tucumán, is owned by the Zavaleta family. The lands still extend over the forty thousand acres acquired by the founder, Don Clemente de Zavaleta, more than two hundred years ago. El Churqui is named after a thorn tree that is not native to Tucumán; certainly there must have been one on the property—but only one—and its rarity justified the use of its name.

The estancia occupies a large part of the Tafí valley in the west of the province. On average the land is more than a mile above sea level, reaching almost two miles in the Abra del Infiernillo (Little Hell Gorge), one of the property's boundaries. One thousand years before the discovery of America, the Tafi culture, which was based on agriculture and pottery, flourished in this valley. The most interesting of the archaeological remains discovered here are several menhirs, prehistoric stone monoliths that probably were used as cult objects. There are also remains of irrigation systems and terrace farming methods, which would have been necessary in the semiarid climate.

The estancia has produced the famous Tafí cheeses for more than 250 years. Hanging from the ceiling is a rustic cane drying device.

RIGHT: *Abra del Infiernillo (Little Hell Gorge) borders the property two miles above sea level. Below, through the clouds, is El Churqui. In the foreground are ruins of circular dwellings used by the region's indigenous inhabitants fifteen hundred years ago.*

The origin of the property dates to 1617, when the *encomendero* Don Melián de Leguizamo y Guevara received the Tafí valley land as a royal favor. A century later, in 1718, the Jesuits purchased this land and established a productive mission that included a chapel and a flour mill that still exist. The Jesuit fathers maintained cordial relations with the Calchaquí Indians, but not with the fierce Quilmes, who would attack periodically from the north.

After the Jesuits were expelled by King Carlos III of Spain in 1769, the valley was divided into several estancias and offered for sale. Clemente de Zavaleta, son of a Spaniard, bought a portion in 1776 with a mortgage of six hundred pesos given to him by the convent at the Reducción de San Miguel (a settlement for Indian converts). On that land he founded El Churqui. Shortly thereafter he built the house that still stands today, with thick adobe walls and a thatched roof. Surrounded by lush vegetation, the house is framed by imposing mountains.

Zavaleta was president of the Tucumán town council in 1810, when the revolutionary authorities of Buenos Aires ordered him to establish a gun factory in the city. In 1812 he was appointed the first patriot governor of the province, a position he would hold again ten years later. At El Churqui he managed a very active cattle-breeding business and raised mules to sell in Bolivia.

Until 1943 the valley had no passable roads, and the estancia could be reached only on horseback or mule—the present owners recall such trips from the capital of the province during their childhood. The trip lasted fifteen hours on horseback if only men were traveling; with the whole family it took two days, with an overnight stop in the mountains.

El Churqui still operates as a cattle ranch, although some potatoes are cultivated for seed. For more than 250 years El Churqui has produced the traditional *queso Tafí* (a type of cheese) made originally by the Jesuits and renowned throughout the country. Clemente Zavaleta and his wife, Sonia Terán Nougués, now own the estancia, where they live year-round. Clemente introduced polo into the region, and his seven sons, the seventh generation of the family at El Churqui, have distinguished themselves in that sport.

Molinos

The nineteenth-century house at La Angostura, a farm that formed part of the vast property of Molinos.

FACING PAGE: *The historic Patio of Honor at the Isasmendi house, with an aguaribay (terebinth) tree in the middle of a courtyard surrounded by long galleries with carved wooden columns.*

Preserved in the modest interior of the church are the embalmed remains of Nicolás Severo de Isasmendi, one of the early owners, who died in 1837.

FACING PAGE: *The church of San Pedro Nolasco de los Molinos, with its characteristic Cuzco architecture, rises amid the low shrubs and cactus in the Calchaquí valleys.*

IN THE HEART OF THE CALCHAQUÍ VALLEYS, on an old road between the provincial capital of Salta and Chile, lies the small, picturesque town of Molinos, with its low houses and unpaved streets. The town is near the Calchaquí river and faces the confluence of its tributaries: Luracatao, Amaicha, and Molinos. The fertile land in this part of the valley, which is more than a mile above sea level, contrasts with the arid hills and mountains that surround it and rise three more miles above sea level.

The estancias that encircle the town were once part of the vast Molinos estate and developed around the house and church built in 1720 by a Basque, Domingo de Isasi Isasmendi, and his wife, Magdalena, a daughter of the original owner. Her father, Captain Diego Diez Gómez, received the land by *encomienda* (a grant of an Indian village and its inhabitants to Spanish colonists by royal decree), which bestowed San Pedro Nolasco de los Molinos upon him in 1659 as a favor from the King of Spain in recognition for his battle against the Calchaquí Indians. When Diez Gómez died, Magdalena inherited the property. Her husband, Isasmendi, became governor of Salta in the mid-eighteenth century. By then the hacienda was the most productive in the region and a major source of food for the city of Salta. Its holdings included the farms of Tacuil, Amaicha, Luracatao,

At La Angostura, ranch-hands work with livestock in the adobe corrals typical in northeast Argentina.

FACING PAGE: *Red peppers are harvested in March and left to dry under the valley's deep blue sky.*

Colomé, and La Angostura, among others. Molinos became the political and economic center of the Calchaquí valleys, because of its prosperity and its strategic location in the northern mountain passages.

Magdalena Diez Gómez died childless. Don Domingo then married Doña Josefa de Echalar y Morales, with whom he had eight children. The eldest, Nicolás Severo, inherited Molinos when his father died in 1767; the hacienda then stretched from the Calchaquí valley to the snowy mountain ranges of Chile.

Nicolás Severo de Isasmendi followed in his father's footsteps by taking up a military and political career. In the Tupac Amarú Indian rebellion of 1781 he distinguished himself in battle; subsequently he became the last governor of Salta under the viceroyalty. Isasmendi led the royalist reaction against the revolution of 1810, and the Molinos house became the headquarters of those who were loyal to the King of Spain. He was forced to flee and take refuge in the mountains of Luracatao, which he had known since he was a boy; his possessions were embargoed and he spent time in prison. A bachelor until the age of fifty-eight, he married a grandniece and had four children, with whom he lived in the valleys until he died in 1837.

Years later, the house was bought by Don Indalecio Gómez, who was murdered on the patio during a civil disturbance in 1861. The surrounding land continued in the hands of the Isasmendi family, but the Molinos house, which had witnessed so much of the region's history, lay abandoned throughout most of the past century. In 1981 the provincial government of Salta began to restore it with the same materials used in the original construction—adobe, stone, and wood from the *cardón* (a common cactus of the cordillera). Since 1987, under the administration of Marcelo Cornejo Isasmendi, a descendant of the founders, the house

PREVIOUS PAGES: *Sunrise at the historic Molinos estate. The main house, facing the church, was built by Domingo de Isasi Isasmendi and his wife, Magdalena Diez Gómez. During the 1810 revolution the house was used as a headquarters by loyalists to the King of Spain.*

Beneath the shade of an aguaribay tree, an old grape press from the Colomé winery belonging to the Dávalos family. Around 1870, Doña Ascensión Isasmendi de Dávalos began producing wine on part of the Molinos land.

FACING PAGE: *Sturdy native* cardón *cactus flourish in the Luracatao mountains, which form part of the Molinos estate and now belong to the descendants of Don Domingo de Isasi Isasmendi.*

has operated as a hotel called the Governor's Inn—the original name of the building.

The plan of Molinos is typical of the houses of the great landowners of the Argentine northwest. It is structured around an inner courtyard with an old *aguaribay* (terebinth) tree in its center, surrounded by wide corridors. The church of San Pedro Nolasco de los Molinos, an interesting example of Cuzco architecture, is a few yards from the house.

According to family tradition, Mass was celebrated on the balcony above the entrance so that Nicolás Severo de Isasmendi could participate without leaving the lookout tower of his house, which faced the church.

Today Isasmendi's descendants own the estancias that were part of the original property.

La Calavera

An old wooden bench in the gallery, where families traditionally gathered and socialized.

FACING PAGE: *The main rooms of the house open onto this large gallery, a characteristic architectural feature in Salta.*

A colorful old Santa Rita bush in the interior courtyard.

FACING PAGE: La sala, *as the main houses in northeast Argentina are called, was built around 1760 by Captain Pedro Arias Velázquez and his wife, Doña Antonia de Saravia.*

THE LERMA VALLEY was named after the conquistador Hernando de Lerma, who founded the city of Salta in 1582. La Calavera (The Skull) is thirty miles from Salta in this historic and fertile valley. A deed from 1760—when Maestre de Campo José de Saravia ceded the property as a dowry for his daughter Antonia, who was to marry Captain Pedro Arias Velázquez—mentions the estancia by its mysterious name for the first time.

Toward the end of the eighteenth century the couple built a house on the property that remains intact today, two hundred years later, with no architectural modifications. It is located at the foot of a hill, from which an irrigation canal descends and passes through the house's central courtyard. To avoid the flooding that occurs when rain causes the canal to overflow, the house was built on several levels so water would flow swiftly through its interior; hence the eroded bases of the furniture. The thick walls are made of adobe and the floors of heavy bricks. The bars on the windows are of hardwood rather than iron, which was scarce and expensive when the house was built because it had to be brought by mule from Perú or Chile.

The layout is typical of that time and place: the main rooms open onto a large gallery supported by columns. The style of the rooms reflects the simplicity and austerity

A small private chapel dedicated to San Pedro Apostle at a far end of the house. On the wall, an oil painting of the Immaculate Conception, from Cuzco, 1700.

LEFT: *The rustic dining room, with its brick tile floor and family mementos, has remained unchanged for more than a century. Above the fireplace, a portrait of General Güemes, one of the owner's ancestors.*

Two of the estancia's gauchos, with their typical Güemes ponchos and guardamontes, *leather leg coverings that protect them from the sharp shrubs in the hills.*

FACING PAGE: *A tobacco crop nearly ripe for harvesting. In the background, the hills of the Lerma Valley dominate La Calavera's landscape.*

typical of Salta. The kitchen is visible from the patio and contains an old oven for bread baking that is still in use.

The small chapel next to the house was built in 1823 with permission from the bishop. It is dedicated to San Pedro Apostle, patron of the region, and its greatest treasures are two seventeenth-century paintings from Cuzco, Perú, that represent the flagellation of Christ and the Immaculate Conception.

During the nineteenth century, several related families of Salta lived in the house. Around 1920 La Calavera was inherited by Doña Carmen Güemes de Latorre, granddaughter of General Güemes, the hero of Salta. When she died, the property went to her nephew, Luis Güemes, a distinguished lawyer and historian. Today his daughter, María Teresa Güemes Ayerza de Lanusse, owns La Calavera and lives there most of the year.

Tobacco, corn, and peppers are the principal crops of the estancia. Brangus cattle graze on the hillsides, where there are abundant woods of *nogales* (walnut trees) and *quebracho* trees. The religious syncretism that characterizes the Argentine northwest is also evident in La Calavera. Each June in the chapel, there is a novena to San Pedro Apostle, and then his feast is celebrated with a Mass and a procession. Afterward the annual branding of livestock takes place along with the Andean *Pachamama* (Mother Earth) ritual, which consists of burying vessels in the earth with corn, coca, wine, meat, and peppers as an offering for peace and prosperity in the following year.

San Juan Poriahú

In front of the main house, climbing vines cover the trunk of an higerón, *a type of ficus tree typically found in the area.*

FACING PAGE: *Surrounded by native vegetation, the three-hundred-year-old main house at San Juan Poriahú was originally a Jesuit chapel. Its thatched roof and thick walls offer protection from the rigorous heat in Corrientes.*

A ranch-hand carries out the time-tested task of burning under-brush to renew the pastures.

FACING PAGE: *A midday rest in the old* matera, *a communal building where gauchos and ranch-hands gather to share the traditional* mate, *an herbal tea. At San Juan Poriahú the ranch-hands continue to wear traditonal dress.*

S AN JUAN PORIAHÚ, the property of Ana María Meabe de García Rams, has thirty-two thousand acres used primarily for livestock. Almost half of the land is covered by marshes, and the vast wetlands of the Iberá Lagoon begin on its eastern border. San Juan Poriahú is near the picturesque town of Loreto in the northern part of the province of Corrientes. On its varied landscape, which ranges from marshes to long, low hills, live *carpin-chos* (large rodents), *yacarés* (alligators), swamp deer, monkeys, *ñandúes* (ostriches) and the nearly extinct *aguará-guazú* (hairy wolf). More than two hundred species of birds have been recorded, including the *jabirú*, the largest stork in the Americas.

The main buildings are built on the crest of low hill surrounded by woods of native trees and plants: *lapachos, ibirá-puitá, gomeros* (rubber plants), and *ombú* trees. A settlement of low houses of simple design, it is well adapted to the region. The three-hundred-year-old house was a former Jesuit chapel. It has small windows, and its thatched roof offers protection from the intense summer heat.

In the seventeenth century San Juan Poriahú was part of the vast circle of estancias of the Society of Jesus. The terrain was particularly well suited for raising cattle: it had fresh water and its fertile pastures formed a sort of island between the marshes that was easy to defend. Part of the old Camino Real, which connected distant parts of the

One of the remotest outposts of the estancia. San Juan Poriahú encompasses over thirty-two thousand acres, used primarily for livestock.

A gaucho herds a group of horses toward the corrals. Plenty of fresh water and fertile pastures in this area make the estancia well suited for raising cattle.

colony, is preserved on the estancia. General Belgrano passed along this road on his way to Paraguay after the May Revolution of 1810.

After the Jesuits were expelled in 1769, the lands belonged to a local Spanish pioneer, Don Pedro de Igarzábal, and later to an old family from Corrientes, the Fernández Blanco. In 1890 Angel Fernández Blanco died heirless and bequeathed the property to a friend, Ernesto Meabe, a cattleman and distinguished public figure in the province. Meabe bought two contiguous estancias and joined the three properties together, calling the new one San Juan Poriahú—which in the Guaraní Indian language means Poor San Juan—because the estancia originally had no livestock. Meabe pioneered shorthorn cattle breeding in Corrientes and brought the first shorthorn to the estancia in wagons from Buenos Aires. His son Raimundo, one of

eight children, inherited both San Juan Poriahú and Santa Ana, a neighboring estancia. An active politician, he was also a progressive, successful cattleman. His daughter now owns the estate.

The Corrientes estancias, including San Juan Poriahú, have changed little over the years. The persistence of tradition is apparent in the ranch-hands' attire, which is so well suited to the environment that updating it has been unnecessary. The gauchos still wear the typical *bombacha* (baggy trousers) and a wide belt; their leggings are made of canvas because they often work in water and the climate is extremely humid. A deer or carpincho hide is folded over their belts and unrolled when they work on foot to protect against rope burns and kicks from the animals. Gauchos from this province also wear a kerchief around the neck in a color that indicates their political sympathies.

FOLLOWING PAGES:
Gauchos and horses in a typical water crossing at San Juan Poriahú; marshes and wetlands cover almost half the property.

Acelain

Ignacio de Zuloaga. Enrique
Larreta, 1912. (Courtesy Enrique
Larreta Municipal Museum of
Spanish Art, Buenos Aires.)

FACING PAGE: View of the
Mozarabic-style house and chapel
at Acelain, commissioned by
writer Enrique Larreta and built in
1924 by the architect Martín Noel.

Flanked by large cypresses, a stone stairway leads to the main house. The whitewashed walls, tile roof, and Moorish touches recall the traditional architecture of Andalucía, in southern Spain.

FACING PAGE: *The Jardín de la Acequia, an elaborate garden where flowing water, floral scents, and striking colors create a rejuvenating atmosphere.*

A MAJESTIC MOZARABIC-STYLE MANSION stands in the district of Tandil, 250 miles from Buenos Aires, in a remote area of the country with a rough landscape of tall wild grass, puna grass, and rocky streams. Rising on the summit of one of these parched hills, which, according to geologists, constitute one of the most ancient folds of the earth, Acelain dominates the silence and isolation of the pampa.

Acelain was created through a combination of the Anchorena fortune and the fanciful, Spanish-influenced visions of the writer Enrique Larreta. The Anchorena family came from Spain to the Río de la Plata in 1751; by the nineteenth century they were the major landowners in the province of Buenos Aires. In 1859 the brothers Juan and Nicolás de Anchorena bought the land that is now Acelain from the widow of Colonel Manuel Morillo. Nicolás's daughter, the beautiful Josefina de Anchorena, inherited the nearly twenty thousand acres of this estancia, originally called San Nicolás. Her husband Enrique Larreta, scion of an old Uruguayan family, added another ten

In the dining room, an oak table and antique monastery chairs sit atop a floor covering made from hides of the Aberdeen Angus cattle raised on the estancia. Lining the wall are anonymous Renaissance portraits of Spanish gentlemen.

FACING PAGE: *The* hispano-árabe *room with its Moorish-inspired, hand-carved ceiling reflects Enrique Larreta's passion for Spain. On the right is a fourteenth-century carving of the Virgin with Child.*

thousand acres to the estancia by buying a neighboring ranch. He called the newly expanded property Acelain, the name of the ancestral home of his Basque forebears in the province of Guipúzcoa, Spain.

The couple married in 1902 and traveled to Europe, where Larreta was stirred by a passion for Spain that would mark the rest of his life. His best book, *La Gloria de don Ramiro,* a novel that recreates Spain's Golden Age, is a result of this passion, as are his collections of Spanish art and the three houses he built as complementary environments for

these collections. Larreta was an innovator in adopting a Spanish architectural style at a time when the important buildings in Buenos Aires were inspired by Italian, French, or English models. One of his houses, El Potrerillo, is in Alta Gracia, Córdoba. Another, in Buenos Aires, is now the Enrique Larreta Municipal Museum of Spanish Art. The third is Acelain, built in 1924.

Larreta started by planting trees, the necessary first step in those desolate plains. He set aside approximately one thousand acres for the park, and in 1906 he commissioned a

Enrique Larreta's writing desk and library, which contains many volumes from Spain. On the wall, a portrait of Larreta by La Roche, a French painter.

LEFT: *The living room was decorated by Enrique Larreta with traditional Spanish furniture, primarily from the seventeenth century.*

FOLLOWING PAGES: *The house is built on the crest of a hill and commands a view of the park and countryside. On the horizon, the desolate Azul mountains.*

One of the stone buildings that house the staff at Acelain.

The bunkhouses, carpentry shop, blacksmith, and stables form a complex built in the style of a medieval Spanish-Basque village.

RIGHT: *Dusk falls over a lone grove of pine trees on the pampa at Acelain.*

prestigious German landscape architect to design the perspectives and the geometric layout of pines and cypresses. Deer imported from Europe thrived among these trees and became a landmark of the estate. Two rocky hills were chosen as sites for the park and the main house. One of these was called *de la China* (China was a familiar term for an Indian woman), because the last Indian woman in the region had lived in a cave in this hill.

Martín Noel was the architect in charge of this grand project. His reputation was based on his revival of an architectural style he called *hispanoamericano* (Spanish-American); he considered the more common term, "colonial," a misnomer. The main house commands a view of the park and the horizon, circumscribed by the Azul sierras. The approach to the house is via a stepped stone pathway lined with pools surrounded by orange trees, laurels, and cypresses. The interiors and the chapel house important works of art and Spanish furniture brought by Larreta from Europe, most of which date from the eleventh to the seventeenth century. Hidden in a corner of the house is a ladder leading to the basement, where Larreta recreated Ali Baba's cave—complete with fake treasure and fantasy characters—for his grandchildren.

Motivated by this aesthetic spirit, Larreta built living quarters for the ranch-hands at the foot of the hill in the manner of a medieval Spanish village, with stables, a carpentry shop, blacksmith, bunkhouses, and a small square with trees, benches, and a fountain in the center.

Many celebrated guests have visted the estancia: King Leopold of Belgium in 1962, the Imperial Princes of Japan in 1967, and Henry Kissinger and his wife in 1978.

By 1940 Acelain's reputation rested firmly on the prestige of its Aberdeen Angus cattle-breeding farm, whose products were sold at auctions held twice yearly at the estancia. Larreta died in 1961 at the age of eighty-eight. Years before, he had delegated the administration of the estancia to his son Agustín and his son-in-law Adolfo Zuberbühler. Today Acelain occupies approximately fifteen thousand acres and belongs to the Zuberbühler Larreta family.

Arroyo Dulce

Philip Alexius de Laszló.
Ricardo B. Green Devoto, *1927.*
(Private collection.)

FACING PAGE: *The last golden*
rays of dusk reflected in the arcade
at Arroyo Dulce.

ARROYO DULCE (Sweet Creek), a stream that flows into the Salto river, is the source of the name of this estancia, which is located in the district of Pergamino, 125 miles from Buenos Aires. The pioneer in this area was Don Gregorio Lezama, who came from the province of Salta. His house in Buenos Aires is now the National Historical Museum and its grounds one of the most beautiful parks in the city. Lezama loved trees, and planted camphors, magnolias, and *paraísos* (chinaberry trees) that still stand in the garden at Arroyo Dulce. Later the lands became the property of Roberto Cano, another wealthy cattleman who was one of the founders of the Jockey Club; in 1878 Bartolomé Devoto, one of the most successful businessmen and landowners in the country, bought the forty-nine thousand acres of Arroyo Dulce.

Devoto, an Italian from Genoa, emigrated alone to Argentina in 1850 when he was only fifteen years old. His brother Antonio followed a few years later. Together they opened a general store, and, thanks to an expanding economy and their innate business acumen, their partnership soon made money. Landmarks on the road to prosperity were their Argentine Meat Packing Plant, the Banco de Italia, and the development of Villa Devoto, a suburb of Buenos Aires. Also important to their commercial activities was the acquisition of rural property, particularly in the province of La Pampa, where at one time they owned 865 thousand acres.

Around 1890 Bartolomé Devoto and his wife, Juana González, built the main house at Arroyo Dulce on the site of an older settlement that was surrounded by trenches built as a defense against Indian raids. At that time the estancia raised mainly sheep and cattle and bred shorthorns. There was also a poultry farm and a cheese production plant.

In 1922, two years after Devoto's death, his widow began rebuilding the house in a Spanish colonial style. The architect, the young Alejandro Bustillo, also built two grand houses in Buenos Aires for the family and one in Mar del Plata. The Norman-style Mar del Plata house is one of the few mansions that was spared demolition during the building boom in that city.

At Arroyo Dulce, Bustillo used Spanish shingles on the roof, replaced the iron columns, and added wings, porticos,

Facade of the main house, built in 1890 by the Devoto family on the site of an older settlement surrounded by trenches to halt the advance of Indians. It was remodeled in a Spanish colonial style in 1922 by the architect Alejandro Bustillo.

All the rooms in the house open onto a large central courtyard surrounded by harmonious arches and columns.

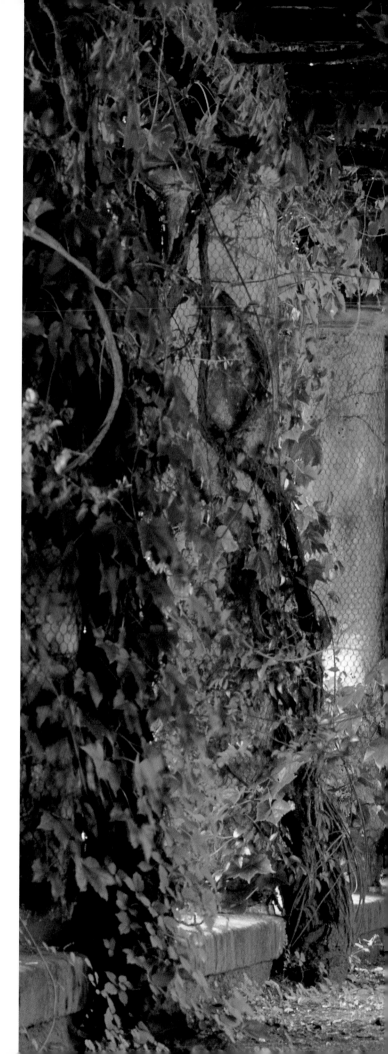

galleries, and pergolas. All the rooms open onto a great courtyard with orange trees, surrounded by an arcade. From the patio one can look through the iron grating of the gate to glimpse a unique perspective of the limitless plain.

In 1920, the landscape architect Benito Carrasco began designing the five-hundred-acre park. Within it are an artificial lake, stables, a greenhouse, the foreman's house, a guest house, and a chapel built in 1928 in memory of Don Bartolomé, also the work of Bustillo. From the main road, an avenue lined with old eucalyptus, ash, and *tipa* trees extends more than three miles to the grand manor in the midst of the pampa.

Silvia Green, daughter of Ricardo B. Green and great-granddaughter of Bartolomé and Juana Devoto, currently owns Arroyo Dulce.

The inviting living room is the most popular space in the house. On the wall, a portrait of Bartolomé Devoto.

RIGHT: *The spacious, distinguished dining room, with its Spanish-style table and chairs. In the adjacent room, a portrait of María Rosa Devoto de Green, daughter of the estancia's founders.*

The swimming pool is a cool enclave surrounded by lush vegetation. Camphors, magnolias, and china-berry trees planted by Arroyo Dulce's original owner, Gregorio Lezama, still stand in the garden.

LEFT: *The entrance portico.*

From the entrance portico, a view of the pampa that extends for miles around Arroyo Dulce.

RIGHT: A wheatfield nearly ripe for the harvest. Arroyo Dulce is located in the district of Pergamino, one of the most important agricultural centers in the province of Buenos Aires.

Miraflores

Carlos E. Pellegrini. Doña María Antonia Segurola de Ramos Mexía. *Watercolor, c. 1831. (Private collection.)*

FACING PAGE: *Facade of Miraflores, built in 1887 for Ezequiel Ramos Mexía and his wife, Lucrecia Guerrico, on the site of one of the most historic estancias in the province of Buenos Aires. Francisco Ramos Mexía established Miraflores in Pampa Indian territory in 1811, after negotiating a peace treaty with local tribes.*

At Miraflores, the flat, limitless plain is an everpresent feature. Carefully designed clearings in the park allow contemplation of the surrounding landscape. The unique fountain topped with a bronze stork was brought from Paris in 1900.

FACING PAGE: *The tranquil gallery, perfect spot for relaxing during a summer afternoon.*

MIRAFLORES is about two hundred miles to the south of the city of Buenos Aires, in the district of Maipú. The house, built in 1887, is isolated in the countryside in the middle of a park with one-hundred-year-old trees. Jules Huret, a French traveler who visited Miraflores at the beginning of this century, noted his sensations of "solitude, remoteness and strangeness. . . . To have the impression that the sun rises and sets on one's own land! That one is the owner of a property as large as the whole of Paris!" Huret also marveled at the refinement of the family who lived in that house "lost in the immensity of the pampa. . . . They expressed themselves in such pure French and talked so fluidly of literature or music, travels

and politics, religion and philosophy . . . that at times it seemed as though I had found myself in one of our most learned French circles."

It had not always been that way. One hundred years earlier, in 1811, the ancestor of this cultured family, Francisco Hermógenes Ramos Mexía, was forced to negotiate the conditions of their settlement with the Pampa Indians in order to establish Miraflores. Born in Buenos Aires in 1773, Francisco was the son of a Spaniard who had arrived in the Río de la Plata area in 1749 and of Cristina Ross, daughter of a Scotsman and an aristocratic lady from Buenos Aires. He had studied philosophy and theology in Alto Perú (now Bolivia), where he traveled with his brother Ildefonso. In

A balcony crowns the facade of the house, embossed with its date of construction.

RIGHT: *A statue hidden in a corner of the park, viewed from the entrance drive leading to the main buildings.*

1804, Francisco married María Antonia Segurola, a fourteen-year-old Bolivian heiress. María Antonia's dowry consisted of property near the Yungas called Santiago de Miraflores, 150 thousand strong pesos, major pieces of furniture, silver, and jewels. In 1806 the couple moved to Buenos Aires and bought Los Tapiales, a farm on the outskirts of the city in La Matanza.

Although they lived there for many years, Don Francisco Hermógenes had more ambitious goals. In 1811, accompanied by scouts and an interpreter, he crossed the Salado river and entered Indian territory, camping on the shores of the Kakel Huincul lagoon. There he could see the encampments of the Pampa Indians on the hills of Ailla-Mahuida and Mari-Huincul. Through his interpreter, he told the chiefs that he was ready to buy their lands from the government of Buenos Aires, but that he would do so only with their approval and collaboration. He promised them a payment in silver coin, and, as a peace offering, he offered to settle there with his family. The discussion must have satisfied both sides, because in 1816 Don Francisco Hermógenes returned to Kakel in a wagon caravan with María Antonia and their three small children.

The estancia was called Miraflores in memory of the Bolivian property; it had four hundred thousand acres. The first ranch houses, built among the newly planted trees, were made of adobe and had thatched roofs. Once friendship was established with the Indians, Don Francisco Hermógenes prohibited alcohol and polygamy, and taught them religion according to a catechism he had written. In 1820 a peace treaty was signed at Miraflores between Francisco Ramos Mexía, as a representative of the Indians, and Governor Martín Rodriguez, representing the government of Buenos Aires. But a year later Rodriguez organized an attack on Indians in Kakel, and Don Francisco Hermógenes was arrested, the victim of a plot by other estancieros who were suspicious of his power. He was forced to abandon his estancia with his family (four sons had been born at Miraflores) to fulfill the conditions of his house arrest in the attic of Los Tapiales, his farm near Buenos Aires. The Indians retaliated violently by attacking and burning the town of Dolores. Ramos Mexía died seven years later, still under house arrest.

Juan Manuel de Rosas was one of the estancieros most opposed to the peace treaty signed at Miraflores. During his government the Ramos Mexías went into exile, and the estancia and the farm were confiscated. They were recovered partially in 1852 after Rosas was overthrown. When María Antonia died in 1860, her son Ezequiel, married to Doña Carmen Lavalle, inherited Miraflores. Their son, also named Ezequiel, had an important public career and recreated Miraflores: he constructed the house on the site of the original primitive ranch houses. He also established a breeding farm for shorthorn cattle and gave the park the shape it has today. His wife, Lucrecia Guerrico, member of a family of landowners and art collectors, developed the social life of the estancia, building a golf course and organizing tournaments with the neighboring estancias. In the evenings there were frequent parties and balls.

The couple had no children, and in 1935, when Ezequiel died, Lucrecia left the estancia to her niece, Magdalena Bengolea Ramos Mejía, because she wanted it to remain in the hands of the descendants of Francisco Hermógenes. Magdalena's husband, Angel Sánchez Elía, modernized the estate and bought eighty-six hundred neighboring acres that had been part of the original estancia. They entertained many distinguished guests, among them José Ortega y Gasset and Igor Stravinsky.

Today the owners of Miraflores are Clara Zuberbühler de Sánchez Elía, Magdalena's daughter-in-law, and her sons—the seventh generation to own the land. The neighboring estancias also belong to descendants of this same founder. In 1993 the Ramos Mejía family held a reunion lunch where they gathered together fifteen hundred of the forty-five hundred descendants of the couple that traveled across the pampas in a wagon caravan to found Miraflores among the Indians.

Ducks in flight above the unchanging landscape of Miraflores. Francisco Ramos Mexía and his wife, María Antonia Segurola, arrived in this territory in wagon caravans in 1816 to found the estancia among the Indians.

La Biznaga

Aerial view of the main house, secluded among the trees of its hundred-year-old park. The property includes a large lake and a zoo populated by deer, antelope, native South American animals, and a wide variety of birds.

FACING PAGE: *La Biznaga's distinctive rose-and-white colored main house was built in 1901 for Carlos Blaquier and his wife, Virginia de Alzaga.*

The park was designed at the turn of the century by the French landscape architect Charles Thays, who also designed the Palermo Woods in Buenos Aires. Today the park contains many cedars, oaks, liquidambar and plane trees.

RIGHT: *The main house was built in the style of a Norman manor by an Italian, Ferruccio Togneri, who also designed magnificent mansions for the Alzaga Unzué family in Buenos Aires and in the country.*

IN THE MIDDLE of the nineteenth century, a staging post stood on the road between Lobos and Saladillo, about ninety miles south of Buenos Aires. Known as La Biznaga (Bishop's Weed), this rural shelter took its name from a small white flower that grew wild in the area. Gauchos and travelers would change their horses there and rest in the shadow of an old *ombú* tree before continuing their journey.

In 1891 Doña Virginia de Alzaga and her husband, Don Carlos Blaquier, bought La Biznaga and six thousand surrounding acres. An avid farmer who had grown up on La Concepción, his father's estancia a short distance to the north, Blaquier belonged to the third generation in Argentina of a family of Spanish origin; his mother, Agustina de Oromí Escalada, was a niece of General San Martín.

In 1901 the Blaquiers asked the Italian builder Ferruccio Togneri to construct their house. Togneri had already designed several houses for Doña Virginia's family, including the Alzaga Unzué mansion in Buenos Aires. At La Biznaga Togneri was responsible for building not only the main house, but also the administration and office building, on whose facade appears the estancia's cattle brand. An old story about the origin of the brand relates that one night a gaucho appeared at the gate and asked to spend the

night. The estanciero noticed the design on the stranger's belt buckle, which looked like a crown. He asked the gaucho whether it meant something, and since it did not, he bought the belt from the stranger and registered its design as his brand.

The park was laid out by the French landscape architect Charles Thays, who also designed the Palermo Woods in Buenos Aires. At first the estancia bred cattle; shorthorn were raised, and there was also a model dairy farm with twenty milk barns and a creamery installed by the La Martona milk company.

Unlike most estancias in the province, La Biznaga was not subdivided by inheritance; in 1961, when such a division became unavoidable, the heirs formed a company at the suggestion of Dr. Carlos P. Blaquier, great-grandson of the founders, and his wife, Nelly Arrieta de Blaquier. With the introduction of additional capital, the estancia entered a new phase. The company doubled the original size of the estancia, bought other estancias in the province, modernized agricultural equipment, and supplied itself with large silos, among other improvements. Today thirty percent of La Biznaga's approximately fourteen thousand acres is used for agriculture, predominantly corn, and the rest of the land is dedicated to raising Aberdeen Angus cattle.

For many years the manor house at La Biznaga was uninhabited, but it regained its original splendor in 1962 when Nelly Arrieta de Blaquier began to restore it, working with the architect Emilio Maurette. She also began to groom the park with the assistance of Carlos Thays, the grandson of the famous landscape architect. Today on the seventy acres that surround the manor house there are many cedars, oaks, liquidambar, and plane trees; the *ombú* tree of the staging post still survives. There is also a large lake and a zoo populated by deer, antelope, *ñandúes* (small South American ostriches) and other native animals, and a wide variety of birds.

The house is decorated with part of the Blaquier family's great art collection, with emphasis on rural themes and objects: colonial silver from Río de la Plata and Alto Perú, including saddles, knives, spurs, and belts; and paintings by the principal artists concerned with life on the pampa in the last century—Pallière, Blanes, Carlsen, Pueyrredon, Pellegrini, Rugendas, and Monvoisin.

LEFT: *From the gallery, the pampa is visible in the distance. The planters on pedestals were brought from Europe around 1890 by Carlos Blaquier and his friend, President Carlos Pellegrini, who used many of them to decorate the Casa Rosada (presidential palace) in Buenos Aires.*

A highlight of the elegant dining room is a seventeenth-century Virgin, from France, and part of the Blaquier family's important collection of eighteenth-century colonial silver from the Río de la Plata and Alto Perú areas.

Above the living room fireplace, an important oil painting, Gaucho With His Wife, *by Raymond Q. Monvoisin, 1856. The silver candlesticks are from the Río de la Plata area and date from the eighteenth century.*

RIGHT: *The interior decoration of the house reflects an emphasis on rural themes and artwork. In the study in the background, an oil painting by Rudolf Carlsen,* A Rest in the Countryside, *c. 1840. In the foreground, an interesting oil painting by León Pallière,* The Procession, *n.d.*

La Vigía

Ferdinand Humbert. Doña
Enriqueta Lezica Aldao
de Dorrego with Her Children
Luis, Inés, and Enriqueta.
Oil, c. 1875. (Private collection.)

FACING PAGE: *The venerable
eucalyptus-lined entrance
road leading to the main house at
La Vigía.*

Facade of the main house, built in 1856 by Luis Dorrego Indart. The lookout tower, a characteristic element of the old Buenos Aires estancias, was used to watch for Indian attacks from across the Rojas river.

RIGHT: *The main salon of the house is furnished with antiques from the original house. Beneath the beamed wooden ceiling hangs an antique chandelier, originally gaslit, that belonged to the Miró-Dorrego palace in Buenos Aires. The painting above the fireplace is of Felipe del Solar, a Chilean ancestor of the present owners. The oval portrait is of Inés Dorrego de Unzué, the third-generation owner of La Vigía.*

THE HOUSE AT LA VIGÍA (The Lookout Tower), in the district of Rojas just over one hundred miles southwest of Buenos Aires, was built in 1856. It replaced the original dwelling (a native rancho) built by the second generation of the owner's family. Inés Dorrego, of the third generation to own La Vigía, did not live there. With her husband, Saturnino Unzué, she built a magnificent European-style mansion on another of their estancias.

La Vigía remains a testament to the deeply rooted austerity of the *criollos* and their fear of Indian attacks. Because it was located near the border of Indian territory, the house was constructed like a fort, with a lookout from which to watch for possible attacks from across the Rojas river. A dry moat for defense is also partially preserved. It is a typical native house: low, with thick walls and rooms grouped around a central courtyard with wisterias, lemon trees, and a cistern. A well-camouflaged basement, intended as a last refuge against Indian attacks, was recently discovered under the floor. The interiors are furnished with period pieces and portraits of the various generations of the family who lived at the estancia.

The park, also native in design, consists of old *ombú* trees, chinaberries, magnolias, small thornbushes, and a long entrance road bordered by eucalyptuses. The building housing the ranch-hands is to the side of the main house and contains the traditional *fogón* (chimneyless open fireplace) around which the gauchos gathered to share old stories and drink *mate*, an herbal tea sipped with a metal straw out of a gourd that is passed from hand to hand.

A historic rancho still stands a few yards from the main house. According to family tradition, Colonel Manuel Dorrego, deposed governor of Buenos Aires province, spent his last hours in this thatch-roofed hut before facing the firing squad in Navarro by order of General Lavalle. The unfortunate colonel was the brother of Luis Dorrego, who had bought La Vigía's 140 thousand acres in 1826. Dorrego,

In this turn-of-the-century photograph, Alberto del Solar, Enriqueta Lezica Aldao de Dorrego (owner of La Vigía), Felicia Dorrego del Solar, Inés Dorrego de Unzué, and Saturnino J. Unzué relax in the gallery. At the small table are the Solar Dorrego children. (Private collection.)

This gallery surrounding the central courtyard exemplifies the graceful simplicity of criollo architecture. All the spaces in the house are oriented toward the courtyard.

RIGHT: *The typical cistern in the center of the courtyard was formerly used to collect water for the household.*

Two ranch-hands share a welcome break and a gourd of mate *in the shade outside their quarters.*

FACING PAGE: *A ranch-hand works with livestock in a corral accented by old native* ombú *trees that dot the property at La Vigía.*

son of a Portuguese man and of María Ascensión Salas, an aristocrat from the city of Buenos Aires, was a great land-owner and a progressive cattleman who promoted the salting industry and became involved in politics. In 1815, in partnership with Juan Manuel de Rosas and Juan N. Terrero, he established Las Higueritas, a model salting plant in Quilmes. After the partnership was dissolved six years later, Dorrego bought several more estancias: El Triunfo, Las Saladas, and El Clavo.

His son Luis Dorrego Indart inherited La Vigía, which was reduced to a third of its original size after the inheritance was subdivided. He died of cholera in 1871. His widow,

Enriqueta Lezica Aldao, member of a patrician family from Buenos Aires, survived him by half a century, spending her last years at the Château des Crètes in Montreux, Switzerland, where she died.

His great-grandsons, Fernando del Solar Dorrego and Javier García del Solar Dorrego, are now the owners of La Vigía, which is devoted to cattle ranching and agriculture. The neighboring estancias, which were part of the original property, also belong to descendants of Luis Dorrego.

Rincón de López

Carlos E. Pellegrini. Doña Agustina Ortiz de Rozas and Her Son, Lucio V. *Watercolor, c. 1833. (National Historical Museum, Buenos Aires.)*

FACING PAGE: *The main house was built around 1810 for Don León Ortiz de Rozas and his wife, Doña Agustina López de Osornio. The house faces the historic Salado river, which marked the border between Indian territory and the land claimed by settlers in the province of Buenos Aires.*

The barred windows of the guest house remain as a legacy of the early days when Indian raids were frequent and Rincón de López was one of the most important frontier forts in Buenos Aires province. The guest house contains an important library of volumes on Argentina history.

FACING PAGE: *The wide gallery surrounding the main house. In the background is a bridge that crosses the creek on the property.*

THE SALADO RIVER appears over and again in the history of the estancias of Buenos Aires province because it was the border between incipient civilization and the "desert" inhabited by the Indians. Rincón de López was a frontier estancia, located on a bend in the river near where it flows north into the estuary of the Río de la Plata. Before wire fences were introduced in Argentina, this was considered an ideal site to raise cattle: here the Salado river formed a natural corral circumscribing a protected corner.

Between 1740 and 1753 a group of Jesuits attempted to establish a mission in this area, but they renounced the task after the Indians proved indomitable. They were succeeded around 1761 by an estanciero who was far less evangelical: the fierce Clemente López de Osornio, who preferred guns to prayers. In 1775 he claimed the land by contracting with the viceroy, as was the custom, to populate the land with cattle and "cleanse it of Indians and vermin." After a period forty years, the land would then be his. A hamlet was built close to the river, with a drawbridge, a lookout, and an arsenal of weapons. Although the property was originally called Rincón del Salado, the name Rincón de López endured in honor of its owner, who exemplified the pioneering, tirelessly energetic estanciero. The historian Carlos

Carlos E. Pellegrini. Doña Agustina López de Osornio de Ortiz de Rozas. Pencil sketch, c. 1830. (National Museum of Fine Arts, Buenos Aires.)

FACING PAGE: *The main house reflects the austere* criollo *style typical of the oldest estancias in Buenos Aires province: windows were barred and the adobe walls built eighteen inches thick as a defense against Indian attacks. Many well-known Argentine writers and politicians spent time at Rincón de López, where the founders maintained a regimen of discipline and efficiency.*

Ibarguren has described López de Osornio as "the embodiment of the tough military estanciero of the second half of the eighteenth century, who spent his life fighting to conquer the pampa . . . and to dominate the Indians. . . . His estancia El Rincón was the core of the southern cattle industry and the supply center for the city of Buenos Aires."

The unrelenting war against the Indians was ever present at Rincón de López: lanced Indian heads were displayed as warnings; there were frequent killings and organized rescues of captives. In 1783 the seventy-three-year-old Don Clemente was lanced to death in an Indian raid, and the Indians' horses dragged his body all the way to the Salado river. His son Andrés was also killed in the raid. His daughter Agustina inherited the estancia as well as her father's strength of character. In 1790 she married Don León Ortiz de Rozas, an infantry captain who had once been captured by Indians. She was the estanciera and the head of the household, a rigid traditionalist who rode on horseback and did not hesitate to undertake long journeys to count her herds or to attend rodeos and cattle brandings—unless she was giving birth. She had twenty children in twenty years, but only ten survived. As the mother of Juan Manuel de Rosas, future governor of the province of Buenos Aires, Agustina holds an important place in Argentine history. Rosas was a controversial public figure who for many years dominated the country's political life and was given the title Restaurador de las Leyes (Restorer of the Laws).

In 1811 the government granted the deed to the El Rincón property to the Ortiz de Rozas. The main house had already been built facing the Salado river. The family spent their summers at the estancia, which is about 170 miles from Buenos Aires. The journey across the pampa took three or four days in ox carts with female slaves and armed guards.

That same year, the estancia was placed under the management of their son, Juan Manuel, who at eighteen had already served his apprenticeship as an estanciero at El Rincón. His sister, Agustina Ortiz de Rozas de Mansilla, considered one of the great beauties of Buenos Aires society, spent part of her childhood at Rincón de López. In 1830, Gervasio, another son, became the owner of the estancia and imposed a regimen of discipline and efficiency that appealed to many of his relatives and friends, who sent their sons to the estancia to learn the ways of the countryside.

Gervasio's nephew, Lucio V. Mansilla, one of the great Argentinian writers of the nineteenth century, spent some time there, as did the future president, Bartolomé Mitre. Gervasio died a bachelor in 1855, and left the 130 thousand acres of El Rincón to married relatives, Casto Sáenz Valiente and Juana Ituarte Pueyrredon. Juana's cousin, the distinguished artist Prilidiano Pueyrredon, painted the estancia in watercolor when he visited in 1857.

Today the six-thousand-acre estancia continues as a cattle-breeding business and is owned by the great-grandsons of Sáenz Valiente. The natural landscape remains in part wild, with *tala* forests and native fauna. The main house retains its original austerity: although the Indians are gone, the windows are still barred and the eighteen-inch-thick walls remain. The interiors are furnished simply, with antique family heirlooms. It is one of the few *criollo* houses in the province of Buenos Aires that has remained virtually intact; an attic added in the early twentieth century was the only change to the house since it had been built by Agustina and León Ortiz de Rozas. The mother of the present owners, Juana Sáenz Valiente de Casares, deeply loved Rincón de López, and, in the spirit of Agustina, she continued to tour the land on horseback even in her old age.

The Salado river bordering the estancia. Near its banks in 1783, the founder of Rincón de López, Don Clemente López de Osornio, was killed in an Indian raid.

Huetel

From the main house, a view of the romantic, fog-shrouded park surrounding Huetel.

FACING PAGE: *Huetel's stately main house was built in 1905 by a Swiss architect, Jacques Dunant, in the style of a seventeenth-century French château. Its European influence and opulence testify to the unequalled prosperity that cattle ranching produced during the Argentine Belle Époque of the late nineteenth century.*

Built for Concepción Unzué de Casares, who remained the property's chatelaine for over fifty years, Huetel's manor house rises in the midst of a one-thousand-acre park. Thousands of trees were transported to the estancia from Buenos Aires by rail and wagon train to create the park at the turn of the century.

FACING PAGE: *Avenida de la Cierva (Avenue of the Deer), which leads to a lake in the park. In addition to a rich variety of trees, the park is home to deer, antelope, monkeys, and squirrels.*

VISITORS TO HUETEL are inevitably astonished by the sight of this stately manor and park in the midst of the treeless plains of the pampa. Many estancias in the province of Buenos Aires are remote, but at Huetel this isolation is heightened by the contrast between its opulent European buildings and the surrounding vast grasslands. The park's one thousand acres contain a variety of trees beyond imagination, and deer, antelope, monkeys, and squirrels can be spotted along its broad avenues. From the house the pampa is visible in all directions through carefully designed clearings in the woods.

This entire estate sprang up at the turn of the century on fallow land covered with tall wild grass. It is a testament both to the prosperity of cattle ranching during the Argentine belle epoque and to the changing lifestyle of rural landowners beginning in the 1880s. Huetel is associated with Concepción Unzué de Casares, who inherited the estancia in 1886, at the age of twenty-two. She built the house in 1905 and remained its chatelaine until her death in 1959.

Concepción's father, Saturnino Unzué, was an innovative cattleman and one of the great Argentine estancieros of the nineteenth century. He bought the land that Huetel

A tranquil garden near the main house.

FACING PAGE: *Statuary embellishes the natural beauty of the park, designed by a Swiss landscape architect, G. Welther.*

occupies from the government in 1860. When his daughter inherited the property there were 163 thousand acres, which she divided into three estancias—Vallimanca, La Verde, and Huetel—to simplify administration. Vallimanca had been the name of a small frontier fort on the site; La Verde was a lagoon where a battle known as de la Verde was fought during the revolution of 1874; and Huetel is the Indian word for armadillo.

At that time, the property was bare and treeless. The first task, which began in 1899, was to develop the park. A Swiss landscape architect, G. Welther, was responsible for

the design and its supervision. Concepción and her husband, Carlos M. Casares, spent long periods at Huetel Viejo—an outpost about five and a half miles away where the original, primitive estancia had been located—while monitoring progress on the new estate. It was a formidable enterprise: 430 thousand trees were planted, including 130 thousand evergreens. The trees were transported by rail from nurseries in Buenos Aires to the 9 de Julio station; from there they traveled fifty-six miles on wagons to Huetel. An orchard of twenty thousand fruit trees was planted in 1902, but when it was barely finished a devastating plague of locusts forced

A marble park bench carved with the name of the estancia.

A path winds through the exquisitely maintained park, a spectacularly verdant landscape in the midst of the treeless plain of the pampa.

FACING PAGE: *Secluded among the trees is this neo-Gothic chapel built in 1909 by Concepción Unzué in memory of her husband, Carlos Casares.*

the owners to replant nearly everything. Today there are several buildings in this meticulously maintained park, including a neo-Gothic chapel, a *crémerie* where cheese and butter are prepared, and an elegant carriage house for the stagecoaches used in the nineteenth century by the Unzués to travel to Huetel.

Construction of the French-style château began in 1905, according to plans by a Swiss architect, Jacques Dunant. It was finished in 1909, and for the next fifty years Concepción returned regularly to Huetel, traveling the nearly two hundred miles from Buenos Aires in a specially furnished Pullman railway car. Guests arrived at the estancia in a special train that stopped at a station near the main house. Among the many distinguished visitors were the Maharaja of Kapurtala and Edward, Prince of Wales, for whom the legendary tango duo Gardel and Razzano performed in 1925.

Concepción was a generous philanthropist: she founded and endowed numerous asylums, schools, hospitals, and churches. Her house in Buenos Aires was on the elegant Avenida Alvear, and today it is headquarters for the Jockey Club. Both her city and country houses, and those of her sisters, María Unzué de Alvear and Angélica Unzué de Alzaga, provided the country with an important architectural patrimony.

Concepción died childless, and her niece Josefiná de Alzaga Unzué de Sánchez Elía inherited Huetel. Today it belongs to Josefina's daughter, Josefina Sánchez Alzaga de Larreta Anchorena, and María Elena Castellanos de Sánchez Alzaga and her sons Ignacio and Carlos. Huetel is the seat of the family's various agricultural enterprises in the province of Buenos Aires.

A group of the estancia's Belted Galloway cattle, with their distinctive markings.

RIGHT: *The crémerie (dairy), where butter and cheese are made for the estancia.*

PREVIOUS PAGES: *The elegant carriage house shelters horse-drawn coaches used by the Unzué family in the nineteenth century.*

Malal-Hué
en Chapadmalal

An entrance to the main complex leads through pastures of the estancia's historic stud farm, whose prize-winning horses are renowned throught the world.

FACING PAGE: *The main house of Chapadmalal, built in 1906 by a British architect, Walter Basset Smith, for the Martínez de Hoz family. Two superb examples of topiary art (English yew, or* Taxus baccata) *flank the entrance.*

MALAL-HUÉ EN CHAPADMALAL is located a few miles from the Atlantic coast, near the resort city of Mar del Plata, in a landscape broken by low hills and streams. The property has belonged to the Martínez de Hoz family since 1854 and has been through numerous adaptations throughout its history. Although it is farmed today, the estancia originally focused on cattle ranching, and it has always been renowned for its horses. The bloodlines of the famed Chapadmalal stud farm are known throughout the world.

The history of the ownership of this land begins in 1826, when a partnership formed by several estancieros received 766 thousand acres under the lease law implemented in 1822 by Minister Bernardino Rivadavia. During the government of Juan Manuel de Rosas, when the law was repealed, the partnership obtained the title to the property. Indian attacks made it impossible to work the land, however, and the partners decided to sell it. The president of the partnership, Narciso Alonso de Armiño y Martínez de Hoz, a Spaniard, was in charge of selling the property. He had been summoned to Buenos Aires in 1792 by his uncle, José Martínez de Hoz, a wealthy but childless colonial merchant seeking an heir. Acknowledging his uncle, Narciso adopted his name and soon became a great estanciero.

The herbaceous borders in Chapadmalal's garden were the first of this type in Argentina. The trees protect the estate from ocean winds.

FACING PAGE: *Subtle colors— white, rose, lilac, and violet— emphasize the serenity of this secluded perennial garden.*

After his death in 1840, his son José T. Martínez de Hoz completed the sale of the land that belonged to the partnership. He bought forty-nine thousand acres and founded the estancia Chapadmalal in 1854. In the Pampa Indian language, Chapadmalal means "corral between streams," referring to the fact that three streams flowed into the sea and formed a natural enclosure for livestock. Between 1858 and 1861 José T. Martínez de Hoz built the first houses on the property and imported bulls from England to improve his herds, but persistent Indian attacks made survival difficult.

In 1866 Jose T. Martínez de Hoz, together with other estancieros, founded what is today the Sociedad Rural Argentina, and became the organization's first president. He married Doña Josefa Fernández Coronel, and their son, Miguel Alfredo, gave the property the characteristics that would later establish its prestige.

Miguel Alfredo Martínez de Hoz was educated in Europe; when he came of age in 1889 he took possession of his part of the estancia and directed his efforts toward improving the livestock. He brought back a great variety of pasture seed from Great Britain and built barns and other farm buildings, making the estancia a model for its time. In 1906, after planting hedges and trees to protect the land from ocean winds, he built the main house with its park and gardens. A British architect, Walter Basset Smith, designed the mansion in an English style. The grounds included extensive herbaceous borders, the first of this type in Argentina, and greenhouses, a rose garden, a terraced Italian garden with stone lions, a blue garden and magnificent examples of artistic landscaping. Miguel Alfredo's wife, Julia Helena Acevedo y Larrazábal, wrote a book entitled *Itinerario de mis flores* (Day by day with my flowers)

Giovanni Boldini. Miguel
Alfredo Martínez de Hoz.
Oil, 1913. (Private collection.)

Giovanni Boldini. Julia Helena
Acevedo de Martínez de Hoz.
Oil, 1912. (Private collection.)

based on her experiences. The small neo-Gothic chapel, also by Smith, was built in 1909; today it stands in the middle of the park, hidden by century-old cedars and oaks.

Chapadmalal's pedigree shorthorn stock, and its thoroughbreds, saddle horses, draft horses, and hackneys won many prizes in national and international championships. Miguel Alfredo Martínez de Hoz's goal was to enhance the reputation of Argentine horses abroad. In 1907 the determined breeder embarked on a trip to England with eighty horses from Chapadmalal; their success in the Olympia, Richmond, and London horse shows proved the quality of Argentine breeding. One of his carriages, the renowned Reliance, made the coach run daily from London to Guildford. In 1909, the Reliance posted the fastest time (41 minutes and 40 seconds) in the eleven-mile race between Hampton Court and Olympia, but placed second based on a technicality. The four grays belonging to Alfred Vanderbilt were awarded the first prize, but the Argentine foursome won a return challenge match.

In 1913 Martínez de Hoz founded the Chapadmalal thoroughbred stud farm. He acquired an excellent set of brood mares and sires in Argentina and abroad. In England he bought the disqualified Epsom Derby winner Craganour, who sired and grand-sired a large progeny of top race horses. In 1919 he made another splendid acquisition at a record price: Botafogo, the legendary star of Argentine racing,

A corner of the harness room, with a display of various bits, and prizes won by Chapadmalal's horses in horse races in London between 1908 and 1914.

RIGHT: A view of the stables at the stud farm, which for many years housed highly renowned and successful thoroughbred racehorses such as the legendary Botafogo. The rose-colored hydrangeas echo Chapadmalal's racing colors.

whose grave is at the estancia. Today the paddocks are named after the great sires that made the stud farm famous.

In 1935, after the death of Miguel Alfredo, his sons and daughter, José Alfredo, Miguel Eduardo, and María Julia, Marquesa de Salamanca, managed to overcome enormous difficulties caused by the economic crisis of the 1930s. They increased the prestige of both the shorthorn breeding farm and the stud farm, enriching the latter with imported sires—among them Bahram, Parwiz, and Rustom Pasha—that belonged to the Aga Khan, and with the top Argentine horses, Picacero, Parlanchín, Seductor, and Sideral. In 1959 the brothers divided the property and the stud farm. The central part of the estancia, including the main house, became Malal-Hué in Chapadmalal ("the true place of the corral"), and remained the property of José Alfredo Martínez de Hoz, who was married to Carola Cárcano. Their children José Alfredo, Juan Miguel, Ana Helena M. de H. de Torres Zavaleta and Carola M. de H. de Ramos Mejía are the current owners. Since 1986 Malal-Hué has operated as a model agricultural enterprise.

The estate's gently rolling terrain includes a lagoon populated by herons. In the foreground, a field of soybeans. In the late nineteenth century Miguel Alfredo Martínez de Hoz planted a variety of pasture seed from Great Britain, making the estancia a model for its time.

Ojo de Agua

The sire Saint Sever, one of the horses that have earned Ojo de Agua its current prestige as a thorough-bred stud farm. In the background, the historic stable.

FACING PAGE: *The main house, built at the end of the nine-teenth century at the foot of the La Vigilancia mountains. The estancia was founded in 1868 by a legendary French-Basque pioneer, Pedro Luro, and remains in the hands of his descendants.*

THIS ESTANCIA, seat of the famous thoroughbred stud farm, is located near Mar del Plata, at the foot of the La Vigilancia mountains. The surrounding hills provide natural protection from southern winds. The estancia's name, Ojo de Agua (Eye of Water), is taken from that of a natural spring that spouts thousands of gallons of water a day. The main house, built in the late nineteenth century, is surrounded by lush grounds extending toward the 250 stables that have housed many stars of racetracks in Argentina and throughout the world.

The sportsman Santiago Luro began breeding thoroughbreds in 1877 at La Quinua in Dolores; years later, at the suggestion of his nephew and partner Raúl Chevalier Luro, the stud farm was moved to Ojo de Agua where the climate and terrain were ideal. Santiago was the eldest son of Pedro Luro, a legendary Basque-French pioneer and the father of fourteen children, who left his heirs nearly one million acres of land. The estancia was purchased in 1868 from the Sociedad Rural Argentina. Santiago administered the estate and received Ojo de Agua as a gift while his father was still alive.

The list of prizes won by the horses of Ojo de Agua is exhaustive—there is not an award they have not garnered. The stud farm always enjoyed distinction for its purchase of outstanding sires and its careful choice of mares, starting with eighteen outstanding brood mares imported from a prestigious English stud farm. In 1903 Raúl Chevalier bought out his uncle and became sole proprietor and director. Around this time he acquired the first great sire, Kendal, also an English thoroughbred, which greatly influenced the breeding of race horses in Argentina. Chevalier died in 1904, and Guillermo Paats succeeded him as director of the farm. Paats also bought great sires, among them Polar Star and Cyllene in 1908. It was not long before Cyllene was described as "the best horse in the world" in recognition of the notable successes of his offspring in Europe and Argentina (four Epsom Derbies and three National Grand Prizes in Buenos Aires). The prestige of the celebrated horse attracted generous offers, but the owner, Doña María Luro, rejected them, asserting, "Cyllene does not have a price."

In the 1930s another sire, Congreve, was destined to great fame. One hundred seventy of his offspring became winners, six in the National Grand Prize, the rest in stake races and other national events. In 1954, María Angélica Chevalier Luro de Victorica Roca added Aristophanes to the string of great sires; he produced the glorious Forli, winner of the most important races in Argentina and later a prized sire in the United States.

In 1970, continuing the family tradition, Inés Victorica Roca bought Good Manners in the United States, a stud with the top statistical record for siring winners and who holds a privileged position as a maternal grandsire in Argentina. Today the stud farm includes the sires Saint Sever, Tough Critic, Espacial, and Firery Ensign, among others, and more than one hundred brood mares with exceptional pedigrees. Nearly all of the land—thirty-seven hundred acres—is used for the stud farm.

The grounds reflect the history of the estancia. Next to the manor house are a great stone corral and a wagon that dates from the time of Pedro Luro. Beyond the stables is a cemetery with old cypress trees and gravestones of the most distinguished sires and mares.

The current owners of Ojo de Agua, Justo J. de Corral, Margarita I. de Corral de Braun, and Julio de Corral, who also directs and administers the stud farm, are descendants of Pedro Luro.

The interior of the house is decorated with oil paintings of Ojo de Agua's famous sires. On the table is a selection of the many silver trophies they have won over the years.

The estancia maintains a cemetery for its distinguished sires and mares; here, beneath the old cypress trees, the gravestone of the celebrated sire Congreve.

A panoramic view of the stud farm and its white-fenced paddocks from the surrounding hills, which protect the property from southern winds. The stable is partially hidden in the trees. Ojo de Agua is located near Mar del Plata, and its undulating terrain and climate are ideal for breeding race horses.

Los Yngleses

Thomas Gibson. View of the First Ranchos of Los Yngleses. *Watercolor, c. 1838. (Private collection.)*

FACING PAGE: *The century-old entrance road to Los Yngleses, an historic sheep ranch founded by a Scottish family, the Gibsons, in 1825 and still owned by their descendants. In the background is the main house. Around 1870 the original thatched roofs were replaced by tiles, and typically Scottish architectural elements were added to the criollo buildings.*

The kitchen, with its sheet metal
roof, is separate from the main
house—a typical feature of the
estancias in Buenos Aires province
during the nineteenth century.

RIGHT: *Above the fireplace in the
dining room is a 1928 painting by
B. S. Donaldson depicting Scottish
ranch-hands at the estancia; their
descendants continue to work on
the property. Flanking the fireplace
are watercolors of the surrounding
Tuyú region, painted in the 1830s by
one of the founders, Thomas Gibson.*

INLAND FROM CAPE SAN ANTONIO, where the estuary of the Río de la Plata meets the Atlantic Ocean, lies a historic estancia bought in 1825 by the Scottish Gibson family and still owned by their descendants. The estancia's name was Rincón del Tuyú, but after the Gibsons acquired it, the natives preferred to call it Los Yngleses (The English) in spite of the family's true nationality.

Sheep ranching in Argentina began at Los Yngleses, and the estancia played a pioneering role in refining sheep breeds and in developing techniques to make productive use of wool.

The region's original landscape—marshes, gullies, lagoons, and woods of native *talas* and *coronillo* trees—is preserved on the estancia's twelve thousand acres, where a rich variety of birds, including ducks, flamingos, storks, cranes, coots, and swans, have found refuge.

On the entrance road a tall lookout tower was built with wood taken from the English ship Her Royal Highness, which was wrecked off the coast of El Tuyú in 1882. The century-old road, lined with eucalyptus trees, leads to the *casco*—the main house, surrounded by the ranch-hands' quarters, the estate's offices, the *fogón*, and an old shearing shed. Originally these were *criollo* buildings, but gradually they began taking on Scottish characteristics. Around 1870 thatched roofs were replaced by shingles and the ranchos were brought together to form a single structure.

The history of the property spans almost two centuries. In 1819 John Gibson, the twenty-two-year-old

Thomas Gibson. Branding at
Los Yngleses. *The woods
surrounding the house appear in
the background. Watercolor, 1838.
(Private collection.)*

Thomas Gibson. The Gibson
Family and Staff, Establishing
the Boundaries of the Estancia.
*The property's administrator holds
a surveying instrument showing the
estate's branding mark. Watercolor,
mid-1800s. (Private collection.)*

The wool shed, built in 1872. It contains the first mechanical baler in Argentina, imported by the Gibsons to pack wool for export to Liverpool.

son of a textile exporter from Glasgow, came to Buenos Aires to establish a branch office of his father's business. He planned to import cloth from Scotland and to export hides and fur. A few years later John's three brothers, George, Robert, and Thomas, and Richard Newton, an employee from the headquarters, completed the Scottish contingent. Newton's son, Ricardo, would later introduce wire fences in Argentina.

In 1825 the Gibsons bought the estancia, consisting of thirty thousand acres plus nearby state lands that had been

settled by a native, Esteban Márques, since 1810. By 1828, the first ranch houses had already been built, and the estancia had six hundred head of pampa sheep that eventually were bred with Merinos. Beginning in 1844 the Gibsons made important strides in wool production: they began to pack wool at the estancia using the first mechanical baler in Argentina and to export directly to Liverpool from the coast of El Tuyú. They also built the first sheep dip to counteract ticks. After a series of experiments and crossbreedings, the Lincoln was chosen as the estancia's exclusive breed, and

One of the many marshes that extend over this region. The twelve thousand acres of Los Yngleses are home to a rich variety of birds; the naturalist and writer William Henry Hudson spent time here collecting material for his books on ornithology.

An example of one of the region's pure native cattle. Los Yngleses keeps one herd of this breed, as well as Aberdeen Angus.

for many years it yielded excellent results. At one time Los Yngleses counted one hundred thousand head of sheep.

The estancia's unique terrain discouraged attacks by Indians, who bypassed the area in their raids, fearing that their horses would not be able to cross the marshes and crab beds. Even so, the Gibsons endured two memorable Indian raids: one in 1831, when they fought off the Indians in the woods in front of the main house; and the last in 1855, when they used heavy artillery.

There were also the legendary but altogether real nocturnal attacks by large packs of wild dogs. At many estancias thousands of dogs were hunted down and killed, but the attacks did not stop. For decades it was necessary to corral the sheep at night for their protection.

Thomas Gibson painted beautiful watercolors, still preserved at the estancia, that accurately depict the rural life of the time. In 1862 he returned to Scotland, and the administration of the estancia was left in the hands of his sons, Herbert and Ernesto. When the partnership was dissolved, Ernesto kept the casco with thirteen thousand acres of land. There he spent his time studying birds, on occasion accompanied by his friend, the naturalist and writer William Henry Hudson, who was collecting material for his books *Argentine Ornithology* and *Birds of La Plata*.

Los Yngleses now belongs to Ernesto's grandchildren: John Boote and his wife Elisa Magrane, Rosemarie Boote de Cavanagh, and Elizabeth Boote de Gurmendi. Despite the current crisis in the wool industry, Los Yngleses still breeds Lincoln and Romney Marsh sheep, and keeps herds of Aberdeen Angus and pure native cattle.

A herd of native cattle and an ancient tala *tree dot the immense pampa at Los Yngleses.*

La Elisa

The original owner of La Elisa,
Former Argentine president Miguel
Juárez Celman, seated next to his
wife, Elisa Funes, and surrounded
by his children, Mercedes, Eloísa,
Carlos, and Clara; his niece, Josefina
Roca de Castells, daughter of
former president Roca (seated at far
left); his daughter-in-law, Matilde
Amadeo Casares (standing at right
with a ribbon in her hair); and
his daughters' governess (far right).
April, 1909. (Private collection.)

FACING PAGE: One of the four
entrances to the main house.
An Italian architect, Francisco
Tamburini, built La Elisa in a
thoroughly Italian style around
1887. Tamburini designed many
landmark buildings in Buenos
Aires, including the Casa Rosada
(presidential palace).

The main house, built as a second home for Miguel Juárez Celman during his tenure as president of Argentina. It was the first estancia in the province of Buenos Aires to adopt a European palatial style, reflecting Argentina's increasing economic prosperity during the late 1880s.

RIGHT: *The dining room, with antique oil paintings from Cuzco and part of the estancia's important collection of Bolivian and colonial silver.*

THE MAIN HOUSE AT LA ELISA was built around 1887 as a second home for Miguel Juárez Celman during his tenure as president of Argentina. He had bought the land in the district of Capitán Sarmiento, about one hundred miles from Buenos Aires, a year earlier. He became president in 1886 through the support of the previous president, Julio Argentino Roca, to whom he was related. They were married to the sisters Elisa and Clara Funes, daughters of a wealthy landowner from Córdoba.

During the late 1880s, Argentina became economically prosperous, resulting in increased wealth in the countryside. Among the upperclass of Buenos Aires the old austerity gave way to luxury and splendor. European-style palaces were built, especially along the Avenida Alvear, and electricity was introduced in 1888. Estancias followed suit. Juárez Celman asked the Italian architect Francisco Tamburini to build La Elisa. Tamburini designed buildings that have become landmarks in the urban landscape of Buenos Aires, such as the Casa Rosada, the presidential palace. He designed the original plan for the Teatro Colón, the city's world-renowned opera house, and many private residences, including the president's house in the city on 25 de Mayo street, which has since been demolished. La Elisa's style is thoroughly Italian; it was the first estancia casco built in a European palatial style in the province of Buenos Aires.

The main living room is decorated
with furniture from the eighteenth
and nineteenth centuries and silver
from the Río de la Plata region.

RIGHT: Columns surround the hall
below the central cupola. The
initials of the first owner appear
above the capitals of the columns.

The bull "Fax," named Grand Champion Polled Hereford of the Palermo Rural Exposition in 1991. The estancia runs a prize-winning breeding farm for dairy cattle and has more than three thousand pedigree animals. Behind Fax, a large shed dating from the era of Juárez Celman.

RIGHT: *View of the park from the gallery. Former president Juárez Celman loved the grounds of his estancia and maintained them personally. The subsequent owner, Alfredo Hirsch, introduced many exotic plant species.*

The 1890 revolution forced Juárez Celman out of office, and he retired from politics. He lived at La Elisa with his wife and their children, where he spent his time taking care of the grounds and the library, receiving visits from prominent national politicians, and reading the reviews and critiques that were published about his past administration. He was bedridden during his last years and died at La Elisa in April 1909.

After Celman's death, the estancia began to decline. During the crisis of the 1930s his children sold it to Alfredo Hirsch, a businessman, landowner, and legendary president of the Bunge and Born Holding Company.

Hirsch was born in 1872 in Mannheim, Germany. He emigrated to Argentina when he was twenty-three years old and already experienced in the import-export trade in Brussels. In Argentina he established companies that were very important to the country's industrial development, but he also directed his energies toward the countryside. He developed the estancias Las Lilas (in the district of Lincoln in the province of Buenos Aires) and La Elisa, where he introduced the latest techniques in cattle ranching and dairy production. Today the estancia has a herd of thirty-two hundred pedigree animals, and its dairy breeding farm has won first prizes in major national cattle shows.

Hirsch died in 1956 at the age of eighty-six. Like the first owner of La Elisa, he loved the grounds of his estancia, which he enriched with many exotic plant species. His work has been carried on by his sons, Rodolfo and Mario. Today La Elisa has more than nine thousand acres and is owned by Sarah Saavedra de Hirsch, Don Alfredo's daughter-in-law. In the ample rooms and halls of the mansion, Bolivian silver sparkles amid colonial furniture and paintings from Cuzco; the architectural features of the house have not changed since the time of its construction.

Harberton

An arch made from the mandible of a whale marks the entrance to the main house, built in 1887— the oldest dwelling in Tierra del Fuego. It was first built of wood and sheet metal in England, then disassembled and shipped in pieces to Argentina by boat.

FACING PAGE: *Harberton lies along the jagged coast of the Beagle Channel in a pristine, windswept, mountainous landscape of forests, rivers, and streams. Its site was suggested to the Bridges family more than a century ago by the Yámana, or "Fuegian canoers," a tribe of coastal indigenous people who were able navigators.*

On the balcony of the main house, a dolphin skeleton and snowshoes brought from Antarctica. The climate in this region is extreme, marked by fierce winds, snows, and coastal storms.

RIGHT: *A view of the estancia's rugged, beautiful landscape and a modest shed used to store bales of wool.*

ARBERTON, known as the estancia at the end of the world, belongs to descendants of the Reverend Thomas Bridges, a missionary who spent his life in Tierra del Fuego. Since its founding more than a century ago, Harberton has been a livestock ranch devoted primarily to sheep. It lies thirty-seven miles east of the city of Ushuaia along the jagged coast of the Beagle Channel, in a mountainous landscape of forests, rivers, and streams. The casco is built on a peninsula, and the property includes several nearby islands where sheep are taken by raft to graze.

Harberton's history is intertwined with that of Tierra del Fuego. The island was once home to the "Fuegian canoers," the Yámana or Yágan Indians, whose ability to adapt to the region's extreme climatic conditions had attracted the attention of European explorers since 1520, the year Ferdinand Magellan first navigated through the strait that bears his name. The Yámanas' lives centered around fire, their only source of heat, and they even maintained fires in their canoes. They lived off of seal, which was nearly extinct by the end of the eighteenth century—the victim of intense hunting by French, English, and later, Spanish hunters. The Yámana replaced the seal in their diet with fish and mollusks, but eventually the Indians succumbed to starvation and to diseases introduced by the Europeans.

Reports of the Yámana by European travelers returning from Tierra del Fuego led a group of devout Christians in England to found the South American Missionary Society to aid the Fuegian canoers. In 1856 George Despard, the society's secretary, settled on one of the Malvinas islands (Vigía, or Keppel), where Indians were brought to learn Christian doctrine and how to farm and breed cattle. Rev. Despard was accompanied by his family and two adopted children, one of whom had been found under a bridge when he was two or three years old wearing clothes embroidered with the letter T. He was baptized Thomas Bridges, and was thirteen years old when he traveled to the southern Atlantic.

The missions to Tierra del Fuego repeatedly failed until a discouraged Rev. Despard returned to England with his family in 1862. Young Bridges, however, stayed on to continue the missionary work. In 1868 he returned to England, where he was ordained and married Mary Varder. The following year the couple settled in Ushuaia, where contact

with the Indians became easier. They had six children, all born at the southern mission, and Bridges and his family—the first Europeans to live in Tierra del Fuego—spent eighteen years there carrying out their humanitarian work.

Bridges succeeded where others failed because of his linguistic ability. He mastered the difficult and rich language of the Yámana (which consisted of thirty thousand words) and was able to communicate with them. Bridges later wrote the *Yámana-English Dictionary*, an invaluable source of information about a culture that no longer exists.

In 1884, following the signing of the border treaty between Argentina and Chile, the missionaries collaborated with Argentine government troops to establish a southern prefecture, the foundation for what is today the city of Ushuaia.

A view of the main buildings at Harberton, known as "the estancia at the end of the world" because of its location at the extreme southern tip of the South American continent.

In 1886 Argentine president Julio A. Roca and the National Congress donated forty-nine thousand acres of land on the Beagle Channel to Rev. Bridges in recognition of his many years of pioneering work in Tierra del Fuego. There, Bridges established an estancia he called Downeast, which he later renamed Harberton in memory of the Devonshire village where Mary Varder Bridges had been born. Her father, a carpenter, built a house out of wood and sheet metal and sent it unassembled by ship to his son-in-law. The house was reconstructed in 1887 on a site suggested by the Yámana as being the most protected from storms on that part of the coast. The few Yámanas remaining at the time raised their tents around the house, where they received protection, education, and work. The Ona Indians, hunters and warriors who lived at the north of the island, also settled near the Bridges family, drawn by their generosity and humanity. Harberton still stands today, the oldest house in Tierra del Fuego.

After Rev. Bridges died in 1898 at the age of fifty-six, his sons Despard, Lucas, and Will managed Harberton, and in 1902 they resumed their father's work at the request of the Ona Indians. They built the first road traversing the island and, taking sheep from Harberton through the mountains, founded the estancia Viamonte to the north, creating work for the Indians. Lucas Bridges recounted the story of his father, Harberton, and Viamonte in *The Uttermost Part of the Earth*, a beautiful book published in 1948 and reprinted many times.

Geese meander along the entrance road to the casco.

FACING PAGE: *A misshapen* lenga *tree (Nothofagus pumilio) is a testament to the fierce Fuegian winds along the coast.*

Today Harberton is managed by Thomas Goodall, Will's grandson, who lives there with his wife, Natalie Prosser Goodall; his mother, Clara Bridges; two daughters; and three grandsons. Natalie, a biologist who specializes in cetaceans, was born in the United States and has lived in Tierra del Fuego for thirty years. She is the author of a well-known tourist guide to the island and republished Thomas Bridges's *Yámana-English Dictionary*.

Since the 1980s the estancia has been open to the public between October and April. The main house is surrounded by staff residences, a workshop, storage house, and shearing shed, all built with hand-sawed *lenga* wood. Rev. Bridges's library is preserved in the main house, along with various Yágan and Ona relics. In one of the old buildings, known as *la casa de los huesos* (the house of bones) Natalie Goodall maintains a collection of skeletons of dolphins, porpoises, and seals.

José Menéndez

A ranch-hand herds sheep on the vast sloping pastures of Patagonia. The main business at José Menéndez is breeding Corriedale sheep. At the turn of the century, the estancia had more than one hundred thousand head of sheep.

FACING PAGE: *The facade of the main house, built by the estancia's founder, Don José Menéndez, in 1917 on the crest of a hill.*

The plans and sturdy construction
materials for the house—wood,
iron, and sheet metal—were brought
from England by boat.

RIGHT: Adjacent to the dining
room is the enclosed veranda,
a typical feature of Patagonian
estancias.

TIERRA DEL FUEGO, the largest island of the extended Argentine and Chilean archipelago, lies at the southern tip of the continent, more than eighteen hundred miles from Buenos Aires. José Menéndez (originally called La Primera Argentina) is on the eastern part of the island, on the banks of the Grande river. Sloping pastures to the north provide excellent grazing for sheep; in the south the land is covered with native oak trees and two species of native birch: the ñire and the lenga. Other vegetation survives on the island only if it is protected by wooden windbreaks against the fury of the cuarenta bramadores (forty howlers), the sea winds that blow year-round.

As in most of the southern estancias, the main buildings cluster around a central square, like a small village: quarters for the ranch-hands and shearers, the administrator's house, a carpentry shop, a workshop, bakery, library, stables, and a covered shed for shearing sheep—one of the largest in the world at nearly ninety thousand square feet. On the crest of a hill in the distance stands the main house, constructed in 1917 of wood, iron, and sheet metal brought from England.

The founder of the estancia was a Spaniard, José Menéndez, who arrived in Argentina in 1866 at the age of twenty. In Buenos Aires he married María Behety, from Uruguay, and they settled in the Chilean city of Punta Arenas, the headquarters of Menéndez's commercial enterprises: shipping companies, mining, and lumber.

In 1878 he bought five hundred sheep from the Malvinas (Falkland Islands). These sheep had been the first to adapt to the subantarctic climate, and they formed the basis of Menéndez's ranching operations on his estancias in Patagonia. His projects spread over most of the southern territories—in uninhabited wastelands he established roads, railroads, ports, shipping lines, and industrial plants. In 1896 he went to Tierra del Fuego, where in the following year he bought four hundred thousand acres of land from Juan N. Fernández and founded his first estancia in Argentina, called La Primera Argentina (First Argentina). He fenced the land and stocked it with sheep from his estancia San Gregorio, on the Straight of Magellan in Chile.

By the turn of the century La Primera Argentina had more than one hundred thousand sheep, not including lambs. On the other side of the Grande river, Menéndez

A flock of sheep heads toward the shearing shed. Currently, José Menéndez raises twenty-five thousand sheep and sixteen hundred head of cattle on its 124 thousand acres.

established La Segunda Argentina (Second Argentina), a 420-thousand-acre estancia.

When his wife died in 1908, the estate was divided between José Menéndez and his sons, who formed a partnership, the Sociedad Anónima Ganadera y Comercial Menéndez Behety (Menéndez Behety Livestock Company), in Punta Arenas. José and his son-in-law Mauricio Braun later founded the Sociedad Anónima Importadora y Exportadora de la Patagonia (Patagonian Import and Export Company) in Buenos Aires.

Menéndez spent the last years of his life in Buenos Aires, in his house on Santa Fe Avenue, where he entertained visiting Spanish dignitaries. He died in 1918 at the age of seventy-three. His sons then renamed La Primera Argentina after their father, and La Segunda Argentina was called María Behety in honor of their mother.

José Menéndez is owned today by the brothers José, Eduardo, Luis, and Ricardo Menéndez Hume, great-grandsons of its founder. The main activity on the estancia remains breeding Corriedale sheep, but in the last few years, due to a drop in wool prices, the owners have also raised lambs and Hereford cattle. Today there are twenty-five thousand sheep and sixteen hundred head of cattle on its 124 thousand acres.

La Primavera

In the park, a modest stone fountain contrasts with the imposing peaks of the southern Andean precordillera.

FACING PAGE: *Surrounded by majestic, snow-capped mountains and forests, La Primavera is isolated in the beautiful Traful Valley in Argentina's southern lake district. The estancia belongs to the Larivières, one of the first families to visit this area in the early 1930s.*

The main house was built in 1924 out of native stone and cordilleran cypress wood, in a rustic style typical of the lake district.

RIGHT: *Appropriate to La Primavera's role as a top international sportfishing lodge, a fishing theme predominates in the living room. Mounted near the ceiling is a twenty-one-pound trout caught in 1982 in the Traful river, which borders the estancia to the north.*

L A PRIMAVERA (Spring), which belongs to the Larivière family, is fifty miles from Bariloche, a well-known international ski resort in the province of Neuquén. The property is bordered on the north by the Traful river, whose clear waters are home to salmon and trout that have made the estancia renowned among sport fishermen of the world. Fifteen-pound catches there are not uncommon.

The surrounding land provides a habitat for red foxes, pumas, mountain cats, red deer, and *jabalí* (wild boar); more than 150 species of birds have been classified there—the Bandurria Baya (stork), the wandering falcon, the Andean hummingbird, the Araucanian and Patagonian woodpeckers, and, of course, the condor, whose flight is one of the most compelling sights at La Primavera.

At the turn of the century the national government offered free land parcels of twenty-five thousand acres in this part of the country to anyone willing to settle there, erect fences, and introduce livestock. In 1904 a Texan, George Newbery, who was employed by an American petroleum company prospecting for oil in Neuquén, claimed several of these lots on both sides of the Traful river and founded the estancia Fortín Chacabuco. A small section of this estate, twenty-five thousand acres in the Traful Valley, was called La Primavera. In 1923 that portion was sold to Sir Henry Bell, an Englishman and former president of the Argentine Southern Railroad. Bell built the house with local stone according to plans drafted in London, but he soon left for England and never returned. His Australian steward, Guy Dawson, was adept at knowing how to exploit the tourist potential of the estancia: he rented La Primavera from Bell and transformed it into an international fishing lodge with a primarily British clientele. The Natural History Museum in London holds several letters dated 1927 from Guy Dawson to various British scientists, describing a strange creature spotted in Lake Traful: "Only the head of the animal has been seen and it is described as being slightly larger than that of a Guanaco, brown in color, but the body which is apparently of considerable size remains under the water." One letter notes that the wife of a *puestero* (herdsman) fired a rifle to scare the monster away.

LEFT: *Red deer, introduced into the region around 1920, flourish at La Primavera, located within the protected limits of the Nahuel Huapí National Park. The surrounding forest provides a habitat for red foxes, puma, jabalí (wild boar), and more than 150 species of birds, including the condor.*

A sorb tree (Sorbus aucuparia) displays its brilliant red autumn leaves.

This souvenir photograph of an outing on the banks of the Traful river at La Primavera was taken in the 1930s. Founder Felipe Larivière, second from right, stands beside his wife, Luisa Torres Duggan; they are surrounded by members of the Balcarce and Ocampo families. (Private collection.)

RIGHT: *A lone fisherman practices his sport in the clear waters of the Traful river. The excellent salmon and trout fishing has attracted visitors from around the world, including President Dwight D. Eisenhower.*

FOLLOWING PAGES: *From the estancia, Lake Traful extends toward the snowy mountains. In 1927, herdsmen at La Primavera reported sighting the head of a strange creature emerge from its pristine waters.*

Felipe Larivière, the son of a Frenchman and of María Luisa Dose Armstrong, an Argentine, visited La Primavera for the first time in 1931. This family, one of the few at that time that dared take sightseeing trips to the southern lake district, fell in love with the place. Larivière spent two consecutive summers at the estancia; finally, in late 1935, he traveled to London and bought the property from Sir Henry Bell. Larivière expanded the original house, built another one for the steward and barns for the livestock, and planted trees to form a park. For the next forty years he spent several months there each year. After his death the property was divided between his two children, with the river as its boundary. His son Felipe kept the original house and twelve thousand acres, and Maurice established the estancia Arroyo Verde (Green Stream), where he built a picturesque house in 1976.

Today fishermen from all over the world come to La Primavera to stay in specially built cabins. The estancia is within the limits of the Nahuel Huapí National Park, where wildlife is protected and only catch-and-release fishing is permitted. President Dwight D. Eisenhower visited in 1960, and King Leopold of Belgium in 1962. Felipe Larivière, Jr., who has served twice as President of the Board of Directors of the country's national park system, and his wife, Teresa Adrogué, spend a great deal of their time at La Primavera.

Selected Bibliography

Argote de Molina, Gonçalo. *Libro, de la Monteria que mando escrevir el muy alto y muy poderoso Rey Don Alonso de Castilla, y de Leon, Ultimo deste nombre.* Seville: Andrea Pescioni, 1582.

Azara, Félix de. *Voyages dans l'Amérique Méridionale.* Three volumes and an atlas. Paris: Dentu, 1809.

Backhouse, Hugo. *Among the Gauchos.* London: Jarrolds Publishers, 1940.

Bacle y Ca. *Trages y Costumbres de la Provincia de Buenos-Ayres. Cuaderno 6°. Litografia de…Impresores Litográficos del Estado.* Buenos Aires, 1833.

Beaton, Cecil. *The Parting Years: 1963–74.* London: Weidenfeld & Nicholson, 1978.

Bridges, E. Lucas. *Uttermost Part of the Earth.* London: Hodder & Stoughton, 1948.

Carreño, Virginia. *Estancias y estancieros.* Buenos Aires: Editorial y Librería Goncourt, 1968.

Carril, Bonifacio del. *El gaucho. Su origen. Su personalidad. Su vida.* Buenos Aires: Emecé Editores, 1993.

————. *Monumenta Iconographica. Paisajes, ciudades, tipos, usos y costumbres de la Argentina. 1536–1860.* Biographical notes by Aníbal G. Aguirre Saravia. Buenos Aires: Emecé Editores, 1964.

Cornejo, Atilio. *Apuntes históricos sobre Salta.* 2d ed. Buenos Aires: Ferrari Hnos., 1937.

Darwin, Charles. *A Naturalist's Voyage: Journal of Researches into the Natural History and Geology of the Countries Visited During the Voyage of H.M.S. "Beagle" Round the World.* London: John Murray, 1889. Reprint of 1845 edition.

Dawson, Guy H. Letter to John R. Moss (typed carbon copy dated Jan. 26/1927). Thomas 1927 A-2, Red Folder Box. Forwarding Letters from Argentina. London: Natural History Museum.

Dobrizhoffer, Martín S. J. *Historia de los Abipones.* Translated by Edmundo Wernicke. Three volumes. Resistencia, Chaco: Universidad Nacional del Nordeste, Facultad de Humanidades, 1967, 1968, 1970.

D'Orbigny, Alcide. *Voyage dans l'Amérique Méridionale…Exécuté pendant les années 1826, 1827, 1828, 1829, 1830, 1831, 1832 et 1833. Partie Historique.* Volume I and an atlas. Paris and Strasbourg: Pitois-Levrault, 1835.

Du Graty, Alfred M. *La Confédération Argentine.* Paris: Guillaumin et Cie., 1858.

Falkner, Thomas. *A Description of Patagonia, and Adjoining Parts of South America….* Hereford: G. Pugh, 1774.

Gazaneo, Jorge O. *Estancias I.* Buenos Aires: Academia Nacional de Bellas Artes, 1965.

————. *Estancias II.* Buenos Aires: Academia Nacional de Bellas Artes, 1965.

Guía Social Butterfly. Con direcciones, unidades telefónicas, estancias, días de recibo y fotografías de señoras, señoritas y niñas de las familias distinguidas de nuestra sociedad. Buenos Aires, 1908.

Gutiérrez, Ramón and Graciela Viñuales. *Arquitectura de los Valles Calchaquíes.* Buenos Aires: MacGaul Ediciones, 1979.

Guzmán, Yuyú. *El país de las estancias.* 2d ed. Tandil: Ediciones Tupac-Amarú, 1986.

Huret, Jules. *La Argentina. Del Plata a la Cordillera de los Andes.* Paris: Eugène Fasquelle, 1911.

Larreta Anchorena de Zuberbühler, Josefina. *Recuerdos.* Buenos Aires, 1985.

MacCann, William. *Two Thousand Miles' Ride Through the Argentine Provinces.* Two volumes. London: Smith, Elder & Co., 1853.

Page, Thomas J. *La Plata, the Argentine Confederation, and Paraguay… During the years 1853, '54, '55, and '56….* London: Trubner & Co., 1859.

Paucke, Florián S. J. *Hacia allá y para acá (Una estada entre los indios mocobíes, 1749–1767).* Translated by Edmundo Wernicke. Four volumes. Tucumán–Buenos Aires: Universidad Nacional de Tucumán, Institución Cultural Argentino Germana, 1942, 1943, 1944.

Pellegrini, C. H. *Tableau pittoresque de Buenos-Ayres dédié à Mr. Woodbine Parish Consul général et Chargé d'affaires de S.M.B.* Buenos Aires, 1831. Original watercolors and text.

————. *Revista del Plata….* Buenos Aires: Imprenta de la Revista, No. 4, December 1853.

Prosser Goodall, Rae Natalie. *Tierra del Fuego.* 3d ed. Ushuaia: Ediciones Shanamaiim, 1978.

Pueyrredon, Gustavo A. *Las estancias ovejeras del pasado. "Los Yngleses" de los Gibson.* In *Anales de la Sociedad Rural Argentina,* Buenos Aires: Sociedad Rural Argentina, March 1959.

Ramos Mejía, Enrique. *Los Ramos Mejía. Apuntes históricos.* Buenos Aires: Emecé Editores, 1988.

Sáenz Quesada, María. *Los estancieros.* Buenos Aires: Editorial Sudamericana, 1991.

Scobie, James R. *Revolución en las pampas. Historia social del trigo argentino 1860–1910.* Buenos Aires: Solar/Hachette, 1978.

Zuberbühler de Sánchez Elía, Clara. *Miraflores.* Buenos Aires, 1991.